ARTIFEX
Sketches and Ideas

ARTIFEX: *Sketches And Ideas* By Richard Aldington

Essay Index Reprint Series

BOOKS FOR LIBRARIES PRESS
FREEPORT, NEW YORK

Framingham State College
Framingham, Massachusetts

Copyright © 1936 by Richard Aldington

Copyright © by Madame Catherine Guillaume

Reprinted 1970 by arrangement with
Alister Kershaw and Rosica Colin Limited

STANDARD BOOK NUMBER:
8369-1438-4

LIBRARY OF CONGRESS CATALOG CARD NUMBER:
78-104988

PRINTED IN THE UNITED STATES OF AMERICA

Author's Note

WHEN presenting a collection of miscellaneous papers, written at different times and in various parts of the world, an author is tempted to make apologies which are always misplaced and misinterpreted. Yet there is nothing particularly heinous in offering a few words of explanation to readers of goodwill.

So far as I know, the necessity to write has not been satisfactorily explained. Possibly it may be due to glandular disturbances or some psychological mal-adjustment. I prefer to think of it as closely analogous to the artistic impulse—if not identical with it—a desire to make things, which in turn is related to the wish to understand and to enjoy existence. The material of writing, and indeed of all the arts, is formed by the accumulation of experiences and that perpetual monologue which is consciousness. Far, far more is stored in the unconscious than is available to the conscious memory, and writing seems to me a collaboration, the Unconscious producing the goods, while the Conscious selects, rejects and accepts with lightning speed. Thus, a novel, a poem, even an article, are shaped fragments of experience, given their shape in obedience to accepted conventions of communication between minds.

As it happens, a great deal of the available material is never used, and yet continues to haunt the memory. This is especially true of the clouds of ideas or pseudo-ideas which dim the

AUTHOR'S NOTE

mental landscape of our epoch. They are unsatisfactory material for the artist, who is concerned with life rather than with mental abstractions about life. Unfortunately, they are unavoidable, even by the despised writer of fiction, who has constantly to weigh the problem of how far people's lives are influenced by the ideas they think they have, while he is further afflicted by his own whimsies in that line. One feels the need to tidy up.

Some of these pieces are mere literary echoes. *The Squire*, *Renaissance Aryans* and *The Jubilee* are the results of reading Charles Waterton, Bandello, and Athenaeus. Others are sketches of people (in one case an animal) half-remembered, half-imagined for purposes of fiction, and then not used. The man in *The Partridge* and the girl in *Thinking Female Extravert* are a couple of cases of Bovarysme, but not interesting enough to justify anything but the briefest presentation. They are certainly not intended to be short stories—merely sketches.

Most of the others are articles, though none of them was written for periodicals, and this book is not a collection of reprinted journalism. I call them articles, and not essays, because the essay is only an article in a high hat. Here I have tried to make ideas and travel impressions a little more lively by occasionally bringing in real or imaginary persons, "scattering a few flowers" as Voltaire advises us. The result may be nothing more than a collection of hybrids, so it seems safest to label them "Sketches and Ideas," and let them go at that. If that is thought to be too ambitious a claim, I can only say that you may call the book *A Busman's Holiday* if you like.

Lyme, Connecticut,
1935.

Contents

AUTHOR'S NOTE
Page v

ARTIFEX
Page 3

A SPLINTER OF AMERICA
Page 37

ABEL
Page 59

PURPOSE IN LIFE
Page 73

FREEDOM OF THE PRESS
Page 85

A RENAISSANCE ARYAN
Page 101

MERELY AN EGG
Page 107

THE JUBILEE
Page 121

CONTENTS

THE PARTRIDGE
Page 135

JOLLY GIRLS
Page 147

LETTER TO A YOUNG MAN
Page 155

FEMALE THINKING EXTRAVERT
Page 165

ETHICS OF AUTHORSHIP
Page 173

WHAT FOOLS THESE MORTALS BE
Page 185

THE SQUIRE
Page 195

D. H. LAWRENCE
Page 209

SEA TRAVEL
Page 227

MRS. TODGERS
Page 237

Artifex

Artifex

HISTORY might change its method and work backwards. It might abandon the theological dogma of evolution and try to find out what really happened. Having decided what is important in our life, it should go backwards and try to discover how these things arose, not arbitrarily "evolve" them from hypothetical origins. Take an obvious thing like shipbuilding. Instead of beginning with Noah or a tree-trunk, start the other way round. We have the ocean liner, the Diesel-engine tramp, the battleship, the submarine, the motor-boat, the hydroplane and a great variety of sailing boats. Is it not absurd to "evolve" all these by a gradual process from the primitive tree-trunk? You can go on evolving your tree-trunk for ever and you'll only get a perfected tree-trunk. The only thing the tree-trunk has in common with the submarine is the idea "water transport."

Instead of trying to imagine what "primitive man" (that absurd abstraction) might have done, try to find out the stages backwards. There was a time, quite recent, when there were no submarines, no metal-constructed ships, no oil or steam power on the sea. Not one of these things is inherent in the tree-trunk, not one of them was a gradual inevitable "progress." What happened was a series of jumps, a sort of quantum movement.

ARTIFEX: SKETCHES AND IDEAS

What happened was a moment of invention in the mind of one man, or a series of such moments in the minds of several men. No doubt there was long and careful preparation, long and vexatious experiments among disappointments and despair. But ships as we have them were not "evolved by the human race," which did nothing about them except to use them without gratitude, or to the multitude of shipbuilders who copied the methods handed down with at most petty improvements—and even those were individual, not group discoveries. The essentials of ships as they now are were due to a very small number of creative-minded men. Doubtless they used the creations of others, doubtless there are almost infinite little alterations and improvements; but in the essential you can name the actual discoverer or discoverers.

Exactly the same conclusions might result from an investigation of less concrete things, such as religion or chemistry. The essentials came from one creative man or a few creative men. Once the discovery is made, there is evolution; but the decisive change is always a jump. And that jump is what matters.

Incidentally, I should like to say that I don't see how evolution accounts for the astonishing variety in the non-human world; and the beauty of it is left quite unexplained. A cuttle-fish and a peacock may be equally adapted to environment etcetera, but a cuttle-fish is a horror and the peacock a beauty. Recently I have been looking at a bit of virgin tropical forest, surprised and delighted by the amazing variety of trees—there are only a few of each species to the acre. Now evolution explains this on the view that each species has acquired and transmitted some advantage over the others which enables it to survive. If you take a huge flat area in which weather conditions and soil are exactly similar you would imagine that the struggle to survive would result in the triumph of one species, that which most exactly adapted itself. On the contrary you

ARTIFEX

find an immense variety. Why all these astonishingly different leaf forms when the one perfectly utilitarian leaf form would be better? I suspect an unconscious subjective bias in the evolutionists, I suspect Bentham had as much to do with it as Darwin, I suspect that the evolutionists were also utilitarians and they wanted the world to be utilitarian. Well, it isn't.

I had read descriptions of tropical forests by evolutionary scientists, and they had all impressed upon me that I should receive a gloomy and murderous impression from the terrible and ruthless "struggle for life" of the vegetation. With entire docility I prepared, I braced myself beforehand. And what did I find? An extraordinary uprush of happiness at the sight of such exuberant life. Certainly, the closed-in feeling, the sunlessness would affect one's spirits, but then we are savannah creatures—came off the arboreal perch long ago—but that doesn't alter the fact that my impression of a tropical forest is not murder but life. Did I look at the strangling parasites? I did, and I observed that the larger and stronger the tree the more exuberant the parasites. And was I not depressed to think of their life-juices being drained away by these lazy good-for-nothing flower-producing rootless vermin? I did not. I thought they made the trees even more beautiful, and that it was nice of the trees to co-operate with them. How do I know that the tree isn't pleased to be suddenly covered with a glorious coloured cloud of alien flowers? And as to the juice-sucking—I observed near the settlements that one of the most exuberant of these "parasites" had fixed itself in great quantities on the telegraph wires. When you tell me how it sucks the life-juice out of the telegraph wires, I'll begin to feel a utilitarian sorrow for the tree....

No doubt I may be quite wrong, and possibly evolution is a fact established beyond dispute. It is a fact, though, that the earth is not a machine for stereotyped mass production.

ARTIFEX: SKETCHES AND IDEAS

Monotony of nature is the product of man. Evolution or no evolution, Taylorism is a human monstrosity. Yet Taylorism and Fordism are supposed to be the adaptation of Science to industry. A Frenchman has observed—I don't say altogether justly—that when Anglo-Saxon scientific men venture into metaphysics they almost invariably take a Protestant twist. The psychological analysts have given a good deal of attention to literary men—why don't they try the philosophers? The unconscious or subconscious bias of "exact thinkers" might then be exposed. With the mould of our minds we take casts of the indefinite flux; finding the casts agree we call them Truth. But the answer is always appropriate to the terms of the question. Ask the question in terms of mechanics and the answer will be mechanical, must be. Relativity is "true," but it is only the mathematical truth about the flux.

There are instances of this subjective bias which will occur to everybody. We are told, for instance, that the great Maxwell (he is always "the great," as Gassendi was always "le célèbre") invented "intelligent demons" opening and shutting trap-doors in front of the flying particles. This was to get round the lugubrious consequences of the second law of thermodynamics, which certainly is depressing to an optimist with a long view of the future. He wanted the universe to go on for ever, just as the dynastic Egyptian wanted to go on being himself for ever. The great Karl Marx was entirely devoted to the subject of economics. Apparently he thought every one else was, for he invented the strange psychological fiction that man is solely an economic animal. The economic interpretation of history (useful as a corrective) is probably due to a similar bias—nineteenth-century worship of "trade."

Christian bias and its reverse side, anti-Christian bias, may be seen everywhere in European thought. There is the Abbé Pluche, for instance, of whom I'm rather fond. This genial ecclesiastic was one of the early "wonders of science" people,

ARTIFEX

a popularizer of the crude biology of the eighteenth century. Benevolent Providence and family affection haunted his mind. He is the author of the famous reflection: "A virtuous old man digesting in the sunshine—what a ravishing spectacle!" Laugh, but don't forget that many an "impartial thinker" is only less ridiculous than the abbé because he is closer to ourselves. Unconscious prejudice for or against the Garden of Eden is not wholly foreign to the learned bickerings as to whether Egypt or Sumeria is "the cradle of civilization." It is important to have the baby born in the right place. I find that although I know little about the problem I have a warm if concealed hope that Egypt will win. Pure anti-Semitic bias.

Pursuing this fancy of writing history backwards—starting from what we find existing and working back to its apparent origin—I think the history of civilization in its essentials might be written in a few hundred biographies, perhaps less. It would be simply an account of the various kinds of impetus given by exceptional individuals to the mass. Cut out from western civilization Osiris, Moses (whoever they were), Jesus, Plato, Aristotle, and all the developments, perversions, and interpretations of their impetus, and what is left?

Two thousand years back bring us to Jesus, three or four centuries more to Plato and Aristotle, a couple of centuries beyond them to Thales, who is held to be the *fons et origo* of all Science; cf. the panegyrics of science-worshippers trying to placate the classical dons. The most remote certain date is not above 3500 years back, in the time of the "great" Thutmosis or Tuthmosis or however you want to spell him. Beyond that all is more or less probable conjecture. Yet, on the shorter and more persuasive chronology, the origins of this complicated human organization we call "civilization" cannot be dated at more than 6000 or 7000 years ago. Some Egyptologists are very decisive—circa B.C. 3500 they say. Perhaps they're right, perhaps they're not. Anyway, let's be generous and give another 1500; years cost nothing. But that is yesterday! Allow five generations to a century (one more than the genealogists calculate) and a line of 350 women (I prefer matrilinear descent for obvious reasons) would show a modern Copt all his ancestors back to pre-Dynastic times. Those 350 would have witnessed the whole development of civilization.

Now, still sticking to what the learned tell us, make a rapid excursion in time before the invention of civilization. We are given a period of tens of thousands of years for homo sapiens to wander about a "food-gatherer," ignorant of the benefits of systematic agriculture, slavery, overcrowding, and heaven knows how many crafts, imagined necessities, religions and clobber of all sorts. Beyond that years in astronomic figures are invoked to fill the period during which the world, the orbis terrarum, was in travail with that marvel—us. Evolution? But surely we are faced here with a prodigious jump? A few centuries after the Egyptians were scraping about with a pointed stick they had built the great pyramid.

My point is that "civilization" was sprung very suddenly on us common ordinary people by a set of transcendent scientific geniuses, and we are still struggling to adapt ourselves to it. A school of psychologists has frightened the life out of us by revealing I know not what complexes, inhibitions, repressions and psychic lesions as the price we all pay for being "civilized." It is a gruesome fact that "we" (I identify us with homo sapiens) have spent much time and energy hitherto in cutting each other's throats and destroying what the other fellow had laboriously and lovingly created. As an aside, let me say that I know nothing so tantalizing as to read Pausanias and Athenaeus—nearly all the buildings and statues and paintings described by the one have been wiped out, nearly all the authors quoted by the other have been destroyed. Sheer fanaticism and brutish ignorant destructiveness—we might have them all. At the end of our meagre collections of fragments

ARTIFEX

of the Greek lyrists we find the proud boasts of the Byzantine, that "at the request of the priests the Emperors caused all these works to be destroyed."

No, "we," homines sapientes (bitter irony!) have not yet adapted ourselves to "civilization." But how if Rousseau guessed right? How if these violences we deplore are not the old monkey waiting to be subdued but the result of this very civilization we think so wonderful? Politicians are fond of sketching pictures of "primitive man" as "a fighting animal" girning at his kind and wallowing in blood and violence, from which uncomfortable state they (the politicians) by their wisdom have saved us, but meanwhile another 50 millions for armaments, please, and not by your leave. The ethnologists and anthropologists tell a different tale. Impressive the alleged facts of a golden age they bring forward. Was Horace right—do we the worse sons of bad fathers beget sons even worse than ourselves? A question to be asked. Anyway, here is our dilemma —with the aid of these transcendent scientific geniuses we shall either wipe each other out, or we shall make the world a desert in the pursuit of imagined gain, or we shall make it an ant-hill of virtuous Socialists. Or will it be something quite different and unpredictable?

Hitherto we ordinary common men have been influenced by theologians and scientists. The theologian promises us eternal life on condition that we accept his definitions of his God and obey him—for he is a great power-lover. What gusto for living must have been in those Egyptians that they wanted to go on living for ever and were willing to go to such trouble and expense about it! But for some reason the life impulse seems to have dwindled astonishingly under the stresses of civilization. Heaven has receded into the background, and the theologian is left fighting for his power by insisting on conduct— he has created the useful little bogeyman of respectability.

ARTIFEX: SKETCHES AND IDEAS

Obviously he never was in a position to confer eternal life, so we may consider him a dwindling type.

The scientist is a medicine man whose medicine works—quite often. Whether he is lofty searcher for Truth (whatever that may be) and produces power and inventions as a by-product; or whether he is a humble messer with gadgets for convenience and picks up Truth by the way—are questions I shan't try to decide. But the scientist also is a power-merchant. He promises power and wealth, undoubtedly in the case of power, but in the case of wealth only according to what you consider riches. He is the father of such undoubted blessings as high explosives, lethal weapons, machinery, economic theories, mechanical transport, the radio, the vacuum cleaner and advertising. However deadly his inventions he never denies them to the militarist, and is brother and bob with the business man. He likes to collect letters to put after his name, and seldom refuses that reward of the virtuous grocer, a knighthood.

Unluckily neither the theologian nor the scientist has acquired much power in the direction where it is most needed—over the military man and the predatory exploiter of the earth and other human beings. I suggest that unless this is achieved, and pretty quickly too, unpleasant things for all of us will happen.

Between the legs of these modern colossi we espy a small dejected and nervous figure. We will call him Artifex, servant of the life impulse, maker of myths, music and images. As we peer back through various epochs we see him dilate and diminish, like Milton's devil or Alice in Wonderland. Sometimes this now shadowy figure mingles with primitive scientists and early priest, but right back at the very origins of civilization he exists, and even before, long before. Or so it seems.

Keeping in mind our Artifex, come with me on a small excursion underground which I have made more than once—into the caves of Altamira in fact. Much has been written and

ARTIFEX

theorized about these caves by people who have never been there, while however ignorant, presumptuous and erroneous I may be, I can at any rate give you a first-hand impression.

The caves of Altamira exist (rather surprisingly) under a bare gentle slope about two miles from the old town of Santillana. In the house by the entrance is a small museum of bones and other objects found in the floor of the cave. You go down some steep modern stairs to a smallish hole fastened by an iron gate, and then step immediately into a series of huge underground caverns, now lighted by electricity thanks to our scientific lords. Close to this entrance the Basque guide shows some half-petrified ashes of a hearth mixed up with limpet shells. He then takes you through a series of chambers, with stalactites and stalagmites, very similar to other limestone caves. Oddly enough, though there is a good deal of drip, the air is remarkably fresh, and in some places the ground seems quite dry. Somewhere or other there must be another opening, though I was told none is yet known.

We now come at last through the fantastic lights and shadows made by the electric globes to the bonne bouche, the painted chamber. The floor has been cut out into trenches about three feet deep for convenience of walking, otherwise one would have to crouch in most places. The reproductions of the paintings, though accurate, give an erroneous impression. In the first place the animals are quite large, getting on for life size, if not life size; they are not separate figures on the wall, but a continuous mass all over most of the roof which slopes down to one side.

At first you see only a vague confusion of black and red shapes. The guide makes you hunker down in one place and creeps away, turning a bright portable lamp to illuminate the roof and not dazzle your eyes. And lo! you perceive that the apparent confusion is made up of most spirited coloured drawings of animals, mostly bison, though there are also boars,

ARTIFEX: SKETCHES AND IDEAS

deer, horses and reindeer. Moving forward, you see how cleverly the painter (or painters) has used the irregular bosses on the roof to suggest the shapes of various parts. More vivid words than mine would be needed to convey the strange power, vitality and skill of these coloured drawings. You can see reproductions of two or three of the figures in a wall-case at the British Museum, just before you get to that large Etruscan tomb. But no reproduction can give the strange thrilling sensation of that painted crowded roof.

Who painted these figures and when? According to one bright theory, invented soon after the discovery thirty years ago, the paintings are "forgeries." We were asked to believe in fact that an extremely gifted painter—who was certainly capable of making an instant reputation by exhibiting—spent days and weeks underground by candle-light, half-crouching to draw with his fingers dipped in colours which he brought in limpet shells. (You can see the mark of the fingers, you can see the shells.) Need we believe such an idiot hypothesis? We need not; even the sceptical learned have abandoned it. Apart from the a priori absurdity of the suggestion, there are many other caves in Spain and the south of France which contain similar coloured drawings, though none that I have seen approach the genius of the Altamira artist, not even the magnificent mammoths at Cabrerets.

The paintings are therefore probably ancient, but how ancient? It seems reasonable to associate them with the objects found in the cave. All these, except possibly the bones, belong to the Magdalenian "culture," which is variously and conjecturally dated at something between thirty and twelve thousand years ago. Let us take the lower date. In terms of our own brief lives that seems a very long time, but it is not long in comparison with the time during which human beings are believed to have existed, too short indeed for any very profound organic changes to have occurred. The cranial indices of the Old Stone

ARTIFEX

Age men are quite honourable. Potentially they were as brainy as we are. And surely it is a piece of vulgarity to judge people solely by their technical equipment. The elaborate arsenal of a modern gang of thugs reflects no credit on their culture.

But we are still crouching underground, looking up at the Altamira roof drawings. Let us get back into the trench where we can stand up, and think about them a little. Oddly enough, there are no remains of fires in the painted chamber. How, then, did they see, and see well enough to make these beautifully accurate drawings? Lamps, candles were not. Possibly they had pine torches, but they would have smoked the roof. Can it have been that the senses of these men were so keen that they could see in the dark? For these caves are completely and utterly dark—well I know it, having been in one when the portable light went out. Part of the very heavy price we have paid for our civilization is the atrophy of our senses. In some respects these Stone Age men must have been far more sensitive than we are. Remember, too, they could have had no sketches or models of wild animals in the depths of the earth—it was all memory of vivid sense impressions.

Look again at that tumult of animals on the roof and try to imagine what the world was when they were painted—six hundred generations back. No road had ever been made, no wheeled vehicle, no metal used, no animal domesticated, no crops sown. Men were part of a living untamed world, less destructive and terrible than the carnivora, though they were clever enough to capture mammoths. The edges of the sea and every river, unpolluted, swarmed with fish. The great forests were intact, the savannahs unploughed, the deserts and high mountains unvisited, and the whole habitable globe was filled with multitudes of wild creatures. That mass of animals on the roof wasn't a dream, it was a daily reality. And those were the people who lived in the age of scarcity, while we live in the age of plenty. (And even that period of abundant life was poor compared with earlier geological epochs.) Think too that the period which elapsed between the time when those drawings were made and the assumed origins of "civilization" is about the same as that which separates us from those origins. Then think what a filthy destructive little brute sapiens has proved himself. Him and his power! And remember that a great deal of this destruction has happened in the last four hundred years—the Americas, Africa, Australia, the Pacific islands, large parts of Asia and even Europe were still intact. How we may bless the foresight and reverent husbandry of our forefathers, and how our descendants will bless ours. Never mind, we have the Power.

Now, still in our cave, let us ask a question which the learned have not failed to ask and to answer in the highly satisfactory way of scientific gentlemen: Why were these drawings made? Remember there is absolutely no evidence whatsoever on this point—all answers are equally conjectural. It is certain men made the drawings, but what they thought and said when they made them none can tell.

One sapient suggestion is that the painted caves were "schools of art," *i.e.*, they painted caves in order to teach other people to go and paint caves. Pedagogues, in fact. Another suggestion taken seriously by "serious" people is that the Stone Age men thought they could catch animals more easily if they drew pictures of them—to draw them would give "power" over them. Now why should the Stone Age men think such an idiotic thing, especially as they lived before organized religion? The first suggestion shows the subconscious pedagogue, the second the subconscious scientist. Because the scientist is a power-slave, he thinks everybody else must be. The stupid and destructive gospel of man's war with Nature had not yet been preached by scientific second-raters and popularizers. I say, if the Stone Age man thought about it at all, which is unlikely, it is far more probable that he thought of himself as living humbly in harmony with Nature than at war with her. He didn't *hate* all that was unlike himself, as modern civilized men do, especially our will-to-power friends.

These things being so, is there any reason why I, in my own uninstructed and amateurish way, should not produce my theory about the Altamira drawings? Subject to correction and all that, my own firmly-held private opinion is that those drawings were produced by—hold your breath—an artist. Our dejected little Artifex, in fact. And he produced them for exactly the same reason that all great disinterested artists have worked. Of course, he may not have been one but several, though that unity of style indicates one mind to me—probably his "pupils" (cf. the pedagogic thesis) were allowed to hold his limpet colour containers. Indeed, for all we know, he may have been a woman—were there not matriarchs in those days? But none of this invalidates my unscientific theory that the paintings were produced by an artist.

The scientist, as I have remarked, does keep his promise to give men power and certain kinds of wealth, without trying to keep them for himself. This is both a virtue and an error—he ought to have kept a sense of responsibility, he ought to have considered how they would be used and by whom. J'accuse—in the name of disinterested integrity scientists have indulged themselves in the sensual sloth of irresponsibility. Nevertheless, they are the brains of humanity. The theologian evidently wants power—hence his intolerable web of sophistries and his grim fostering of prejudice and ignorance. His offer of eternal life is evidently a frantic effort to outbid any competitors. Nobody knows what happens after death, except the obvious and striking fact that the living organism ceases to be one. The theologian knows nothing more than we do, and his offer is a bit of cheek—a manifest gold brick, in fact.

And now what had and has Artifex to offer—the painter of those animals twelve thousand years ago, and his contemporary and unfortunately too often degenerate descendant? I suggest that the answer is "immediate life" (hence, by the bye, the theologian's outbidding) and also "determination of values." In the latter function, however, he has numerous competitors, including all women. All through the ages Artifex has been trying to show men the "wonder" and the "beauty" of the world they live in; he has tried truly to give "more life" by showing the excellence of all that lives; he has invited men to come out of their egotism to perceive and reverence the mysterious differences of things, their "otherness"; he has given them "experiences" (and what is life if not the experience of consciousness?) actual and imaginary, amusing and tragical, moral and immoral, sometimes well and sometimes feebly, in form, colour, sound and words. He has turned the world of things and of human beings from a mere environment noticed only for the immediate purposes of existence into a deeply-significant and glorious pageant to be enjoyed and revered. And in so doing he has, as we pedantically put it, "conferred values."

Believe me, he has never tried to make a duplicate world, to photograph it, except when he has been tempted or even forced to do so by the clamorous bad taste of audience or master. Nor is his method rightly called either abstraction, conventionalizing or deformation. He selects, but he does not abstract—a scientist does that—he is concrete; he is not a conventionalizer, he is an explorer and adventurer; and he does not deform, he forms. His method is "essentializing," the essential forms and "modes of being" of life, including of course his own, are what he chooses in order to enrich experience. So I claim for Artifex that he is the genuine "life-giver." His art is a religion that existed before religion. He is an unconscious hylozoist. His animism stops short of magic and superstition. He does not say "bow down and worship them"—the theologian says that—he says "revere and enjoy them." True, he has been

ARTIFEX

forced to act as propagandist by king and priest, warrior and even merchant, but he has nearly always slipped his own message in as well. In the cave of Altamira he was free, and perhaps some day he may be free again. His true function is to be no man's slave or trumpeter, but a servant of the life impulse.

I now propose that we adjourn from the cave to the wine-shop in Santillana. But before we go, *un moment de recueillement*. This is one of Man's sacred places. That unknown artist lived before there were any kings or priests or merchants or scientists or warriors. It is fashionable to think of him as a brute and a savage, but let us think of what he did here. He made a tremendous discovery, one of the first great "jumps" in human effort. He and his like were the far-off ancestors of all the arts, without which our lives would indeed be dull and brutish. He can have had no reward; what he did, he did for its own sake, for life's sake. Let us hope that his little group of wanderers learnt dimly from him that the world about them —that virgin world which seems so strange and far-off to us— was something more than a place where food was gathered. We shall never know who he was, and yet he still speaks to us across twelve millennia, over all human history.

As we walk back to Santillana I shall be unable to ask you to look at any of the animals we saw in the cave. They have been improved out of existence. But the people of Santillana still live among animals; in fact the whole place is a picturesque cow byre, for the animals live in the houses with the people. To see a bison we should have to go to Canada or Yellowstone Park or to the dejected specimens imprisoned miserably in Zoos. So let us take one of the Santillana bulls, which still enjoy the relative freedom of the fields. And let us imagine that as we look at the bull, we are joined by a Theologian, a Business Man, a Scientist, and an Artist, a not too degraded descendant of our

ARTIFEX: SKETCHES AND IDEAS

cave Artifex. And let us ask them what they see in the bull. The Theologian will say it is a splendid animal, splendid. We ought to thank God (his God) for having created such a splendid food supply for our use. (He will not of course mention that bulls existed for tens of thousands of years before there were any men to eat them.) We have souls to be saved to everlasting life, but bulls have no souls—they cannot worship God and put sixpence in the plate. All things were created for man's use, and it is heretical to suppose that man has any duties to the lower animals. They have no spiritual life. The Israelites were punished by God for worshipping a golden calf —the gold should have gone to the temple. One splendid thing about bulls is that, by God's blessing, they enable the farmer to pay his tithes. There will be no bulls in Heaven, unless the Evangelist is allowed to keep his as a pet.

If our Business Man is of the predatory kind he will know a lot about Stock Exchange bulls, and mighty little about bulls in fields. But let us assume that he is an honest-to-God merchant, who surely has a useful necessary and honourable part to play in life. He will at once "value" the bull for us, tell us what it is "worth" in pesetas or pounds or some other immutably fixed currency. He will talk about markets and profits, estimate what stock might be bred, discuss what can be "done" with the dead flesh, horns, bones, hide. He will in fact have pretty much the same idea of a bull as the food-gatherers up in the cave had before Artifex came along. And if he is a go-ahead progressive man he will express his dissatisfaction with the Santillana unbusinesslike peasant methods and indeed with bulls generally as a slow, cumbersome, unsatisfactory basis for business— what he hopes is that our Scientific friend will give (or sell for a totally inadequate share of the profits) a method of producing an "acceptable substitute" which can be mass produced and sold in tins.

Now is the turn of our Scientist, about whom we must make

ARTIFEX

the unlikely supposition that he is not a specialist but a walking compendium of "what is known." He will have so much that is interesting to tell us, even when it is conjecture, that I shall not attempt to summarize it. Starting with the geological history of bulls, he will carry us on to zoology, anatomy, genetics, Mendelian laws, animal behaviour, statistical averages and the like. He will prove to us that Science can "improve" the breed by judicious incest, the "improvement" consisting in making the animal more profitable to our Business friend. He will "work out" the rations of our bull to a centigramme, and estimate the milk-production of the bull's daughters within a margin of error of ten gallons annually. While estimating the exact number of calories the carcase would furnish, he will astonish us by explaining how it may profitably be turned into glue. And he will inveigh against the stupidity of the Santillana peasants, who persist in eating their beef tender, when they might export it scientifically chilled and toughened at great expense to the Lotophagoi or vegetarians of Thule.

Meanwhile what has our penurious Artifex been doing? You will observe that his linen is none of the freshest—indeed it is Japanese cotton—and that the seat of his bags is decidedly shiny. With an odd mixture of defiance and cringing—he suspects we have a few idle guineas in our pockets—he presents us with a sketch. What has he done? With a few trained essential lines in coloured chalk he puts before us the one thing our other friends have overlooked—the mysterious living bull, his massive hotly sexual bull life. He is evidently recommending us to enjoy the majesty and mystery of this phallic animal, for whom the Theologian is wistfully devising pudic pants.

The sketch passes from hand to hand. Premising that he knows nothing about Art but does know what he likes, the Business Man asks if the left foreleg is not a little out of drawing, and professes disapproval of reproducing a black beast in red chalk. The Theologian informs us that by a recent de-

ARTIFEX: SKETCHES AND IDEAS

cision of Authority no animal may be represented in Consecrated Buildings. The artistic qualities of a sacred image are of no importance so long as it conduces to edification and devotion—*vide* the basilica of Jeanne d'Arc at Domremy, or rather don't, it's a horror. (Now that art has ceased to possess propaganda value, the Theologian abandons it to the devil.) As to our Scientist, in whom we have been hoping to find a valuable ally since his interests are the complement of our own—he deserts us by remarking that it is pretty but what does it *mean?* What do we mean by meaning and what is the meaning of meaning? We are chilled to the spine by the suspicion that he believes in Scientific Criticism.

Having some profitable business in the capital to transact, the Scientist now makes for the railway station, arm-in-arm with the Theologian and the Business Man—a triumvirate of self-importance. We begin to sympathize with the Barcelona anarchists. . . .

It is very far from my intention to make any excursion into that luckless bog of aesthetics which has already engulfed so many acute disputants, and I am equally incompetent in the matter of a history of art. These things must be left to the learned. Yet there are many activities of Artifex throughout the ages which might be discussed over our wine. We might, for instance, take a modern printed book, and trace back the history of printing to the Chinese, and of writing to the earliest hieroglyphic and cuneiform, and that undeciphered Aegean script; thence to the Dordogne caves where we shall find Artifex already dealing in symbols. The white hands in the Cabrerets cave turn up as a pottery mark in pre-dynastic Egypt, are found in the quite recent wall-drawings of the Bushmen, while you may see the hand of Fatima still worn as an amulet in north Africa.

Symbolism alone would occupy us for hours. It is a mental attitude almost lost to mankind but once extremely potent and

ARTIFEX

valuable; it is the picture-thinking of the religion of wonder and reverence for the living world. That it degenerated into magic and superstition is unfortunate and only too true, but have not all religions their superstitions, is there not even a superstition of Science? Common minds always mistake the true purpose of every non-materialist activity, and crave for the sensational. There has always been an appetite for the false marvellous in place of the true wonder; and there have always been found traitors (another trahison des clercs) to exploit it for their own profit and power. The true value of the work of art, whether symbolical or not, lies I believe in the experience communicated; and the endless discussions of aesthetes really circle round the quality of the experience and the sensitiveness or insensitiveness of the percipient. Crude sensibilities experience nothing whatever, and yet have to find some explanation for the "value" put by others on the work of art. Our Business friend is impressed if he is told that a Titian is "worth" a million dollars; he would want to jail a living Titian. The Latin crusaders found Constantinople full (papai!) of Greek bronzes. After relating various idiot tales about the "miracles" of speech and whatnot performed by these idols (see the memoirs of Robert de Clari), they melted them down to coin ha'pennies, thereby demonstrating the spirituality of their natures. Their methods were a little franker and rougher than our Business friend's, but their aims and perceptions fairly similar.

If you don't possess the particular kind of sensibility which delights in symbolism (don't confuse with allegory, that debased and boring ingenuity) then there is not much good trying to explain it. Every night we lie down to sleep with no particular feeling about it, except for a comfortable bed. The Egyptian laid his head on a curved rest, supported by two kneeling women who meant The Day that is Gone and The Day that is to Come. Or the figures might be two guardian lions with the same meaning. Or the rest might be in the shape of Nut, the goddess of Night. In any case the Egyptian was reminded of the mystery and wonder of night and sleep, and rested his head between day and day. You think that childish and absurd? But suppose we say that your dead, mechanical, unsacred world is not only childish and absurd, but obtuse and hoggish? It's a question of whether you hog your life, or feel it delicately in all its modes and moments.

The murder of this sensibility, the destruction of this piety to the living world by the combined forces of the Theologian, the Scientist and the Business Man have resulted in the desperately disfigured earth we see today and the worse disfigurement we shall see tomorrow. If the Scientist had allied himself with Artifex instead of pandering to the Business Man and the Man in Power. . . . But it is now too late, we must dree our weird, and it will be mighty unpleasant. Yet there was no reason why the power of Science should not have been wisely used. The Black Country wasn't "inevitable," the dreary slums and suburbs weren't "inevitable." You wanted them; you've got them; now get out of them—if you can. Go to Marseille harbour. For miles the smooth blue water is foul with eddies of black grease and every filth imaginable. Is it "inevitable?" Not at all, you *want* to pollute the sea, because the Theologian has taught you to despise it as "unspiritual," and the Scientist has taught you it is merely salt water and that you have "power" over it. What practically is the "power" of science able to produce? Transport and machine-made objects. Kipling told a big lie when he said "civilization is transportation"—civilization is not what carries but the thing carried. And Georges Duhamel has put it well: If civilization exists, it is not in all this clobber (cette pacotille) but in the hearts of men and women.

"Tell me, O Muse, of the dear child of Hermes, goat-footed, two-horned, castanet-lover, wanderer in woodland valleys with the dancing nymphs who glide on the steep mountain, crying after Pan, shepherd-god, long-haired, uncombed. His are the snow-covered peaks and the mountain ridges and the rocky places, and he moves through the tangled copses, sometimes charmed by the soft rivers, and sometimes he mounts among the huge crags and from the highest point looks down upon the herds. He runs among the glittering mountains, sharp-eyed he rushes with the wild things among the hills. At night he plays softly on his reed-pipe, and none makes sweeter melody, not even the nightingale who in the leaves of many-flowering spring laments and pours out honey-sweet song. Then the clear-voiced nymphs dance before him on swift feet, singing by the dark waters of the stream, Echo calls from the mountain, and the god dances with them, now on one side, now on the other, now in the midst, wearing the fur of a spotted lynx, delighting in clear song in a soft meadow where the crocus and sweet-breathing hyacinth flower scattered in the grasses."

It is said by the learned—I don't know on what grounds—that this "Homeric" hymn formed part of an ancient ritual. And ritual is the attempt to systematize the experiences of sensibility for the benefit of the insensitive, to suggest a way of life to them. Well, you will not find that kind of sensibility to the mystery and beauty of the living world either in Hymns A. and M., or in the text-books of physics or in the subtle meanderings of the metaphysicians. You may call it "senti-*men*tal," if you choose, but that is only your way of admitting that you are inaccessible to such feelings.

But it is evidently time I stood you that drink in the wine-shop. Don't hang back because you see it is a "rough peasant" place with peasants drinking, but remember as we enter to raise your hat and say in a man's voice: "Señores!" Now let us sit at the table by the door where we can look into the village.

ARTIFEX: SKETCHES AND IDEAS

Don't be nervous! These silent rough-looking men are caballeros, proud that their ancestors have never been serfs and fought the Moor for every inch of their farms. Doubtless Señor Puig from Barcelona, Señorito Fulano from Santander, and Señor Mosco the socialist deputy in Madrid would have plenty to say against them, but so long as we behave as gentlemen, they will treat us with a courtesy you won't find in Kensington. They are certainly curious about us, but they won't show it; here you'll have no staring Italian impertinence, no German truculence or cockney giggle at the stranger. But remember—if you wish to be treated as a caballero, behave like one. Don't *you* stare or giggle or be truculent—there's a knife in each of those black sashes.

Let me brag a little about this wine-shop. Look at the table. It is made of plain heavy wood, but scrubbed until it is nearly as white as paper, which, entre nous, gives me more reassurance of cleanliness than the cat-lick of a damp rag on a pseudo-marble table from the over-worked waitress of a London bun-hall. The glasses and wine-decanter have been polished until they are really like crystal—which I admit you won't find in most wine-shops or in many private houses. Since it is not good to drink wine on an empty stomach I have ordered such trifles as a poor house can provide—large olives from Andalusia, anchovies from the Mediterranean just washed in wine to take the salt off, bread from the great upland of Castile and butter from the cow in the yard. Common stuff, but authentic, no "acceptable substitute" here. The wine too is common but made from grapes—I saw it poured from the foreleg of a goat-skin, which, I assure you, is a better guarantee than the florid labels on those bottles of scientific concoction with which your liver will be afflicted in hotels, and for which you will pay about ten times as much.

The moral of all this? Only that I should prefer my food and drink to come to me direct from the ignorant peasant, without any expert assistant from the scientific substituter and preserver or the highly enlightened company promoter. I don't mind taking what comes, so long as it is genuine, in any country; but I don't like countries which "produce for the world market" and in consequence have to live out of tins. If we had not lost all sense of living we should know that a fresh herring is better than stale "scientifically preserved" caviare and lobsters poisoned with engine grease. That's all.

Now we can sip our wine in the cool of the evening, and watch the peasants coming home with their animals. The village is old and tumbly, the streets ill-paved and there are no great shakes in the way of sewers. On the other hand, it is evident that Artifex was consulted about the buildings. Every one is pleasantly shaped, and all together they make a harmony, a modestly beautiful setting for modest lives. Admittedly one or two of the ancient noblesse rather over-advertised their quality in those huge stone armorials; but, odd as it may seem, I can more easily admit them than ill-designed posters vaunting the perfections of substitute jams and pickles. Here is a contrast to that "other Eden" of the Business Man and the Scientist from which we come! There, as you know, the streets are made of concrete smeared with asphalt, and are everlastingly being dug up with hideous din of concrete-crunchers—in order that they may be relaid. I suppose once in fifty years or a century is enough here. If you made friends with the municipal employees I dare say they would allow you to enjoy a visit to the admirable sewers in that royal seat of Mars; but you will not find that the buildings give you that happiness which a walk down these two streets here never fails to give me. Indeed, if there were any such phoenix in the world as a person who felt too happy, I should advise him to perlustrate the streets of a few English industrial towns. That, with gin and journalism, would soon bring him to a decent level of misery.

ARTIFEX: SKETCHES AND IDEAS

Here is the paradox of our time. In this and many another old village you have graciousness, beauty, a sense of human dignity, along with great inconveniences and ignorances. The people who live in them today certainly could not create them—that came from the past, and is perishing. Soon these places will be unfit for human habitation. On the other hand, while modern towns are extended at enormous expense they, also, in a very real sense, are unfit for human habitation. They may be all very well for insentiate robots, but they seem to combine the disadvantages of the old and new, with few of the advantages. They are ugly as sin, and depressing as economics. . . .

But it is evident that I am involving myself in one of those discussions *de gustibus* to which there is no end. The energy of men is prodigious; their power, as we are assured, vastly greater than it ever was; therefore if they live dull lives in banal surroundings, they must like dullness and banality. It is related of the Celts—I think by Caesar—that many among them would commit suicide for a pint of wine and a few shillings to scatter among their admiring friends and survivors. Others today will commit matrimony intrepidly for even more slender rewards. *De gustibus* . . . there is no accounting for the animal. I can easily imagine an industrialist, fired with civic pride and exultation, gazing upon the human mews he has created, and crying: I can see nothing wrong here! That, of course, is the point—he can't see.

But how of *la beauté moderne?* Is it not perhaps the fact that we malcontents, *laudatores temporis acti,* fail to see the beauties of Science and Industry! What could be lovelier than a dissected frog, more inspiring than the music of a rock drill, more of a clarion call to fire the blood than the language of advertisements? If Vesuvius under its cloud-cap is grand, why not Sheffield which lives under an eruption of smuts and looks like

ARTIFEX

a Pompeii of dealers in old iron? Can you not imagine some northern Huysmans, some good companion off his rocker, snooping along the ways of Middlesborough, *à la récherche de la beauté moderne?* Indeed I have thought myself that something might be done with that immense bottle of stout which so significantly decorates the span of the railway bridge over the main street. But what of the people, butchered to make an aesthete's holiday? What, indeed, of the people! I think of those back streets and shiver.

Certainly there is art now, but it is the art of hyperaesthesia, the art of exasperated neurasthenics. The latest aesthetic giggle, the newest *petit frisson*—anything, anything to seem original. The music of atonality, the painting and sculpture of superrealism, the literature of the stream of consciousness, the aestheticism of concrete and cocktails—neurasthenia and self-destruction. Intellectual snobbishness is the very essence of its appeal to the gangs and cliques of Paris and London. If it were not inaccessible to common sense they would not want it. And if it does show talent, why then lament thereat? Why should we admire these self-conscious perversities, this feeble sodomizing of the Muses? As for the swinish multitude—abandon them to the venal, the vulgar and the mediocre.

The plight of the arts is like the alleged political plight of France—congestion at the centre, starvation at the extremities. The arts are imprisoned like Danaës, waiting for a shower of gold which doesn't come. Three blocks away from the rendezvous of the cliques you would not know art existed. There is intense competition for the favour of a very small audience which is naturally jaded by the perpetual demands made on its attention, and therefore needs the stimulus of the extraordinary—anything to startle or amuse. The sensationalism of the art-mob is the snobbish brother of the newspaper mob's sensationalism. Over-production for a public of snobs inevitably results not only in perversities to attract attention,

ARTIFEX: SKETCHES AND IDEAS

but in the vices of intrigue, back-scratching and malignant disparagement of rivals. I have thought and said harsh things of Business Men, but I must say I have never known them talk of other men with anything approaching the crapulous spitefulness of artists. It is gang warfare with the tongue. . . . But I have said enough. There is nothing to do about these people but avoid them.

Side by side with this, and not infrequently recruited from its rank, is the army of art as a business—or rather, the chaos. And there is nothing to be done about chaos either.

After this, let us moisten the lips, and begin again. I invite your attention to the European peasant. . . . Taking the chorus of jeers for granted, I proceed. There seems to be a notion that the peasant was invented by the Roman Catholic Church, and so (according to their prejudices) one set crack him up to the skies as God's good man, while the other denounces him as a bestial obscurantist. I take leave to point out that he is co-eval with "civilization," that hitherto any community has been impossible without him. He may be superseded by machines, but he was in fact invented by the old agricultural civilizations of Egypt and Mesopotamia, and thence spread over the world with their "culture." And if you're not a diffusionist, it doesn't matter—put it that similar circumstances produce similar results. My point is that when the Church took over in the fourth century, the peasant had already been long established. He was the toughest nut the Church had to crack, and I'm not sure it wasn't the Church which cracked.

Both sides in this curious peasant controversy are right and wrong. The peasant has virtues, and he has faults. He may be Catholic or Protestant, but he is very seldom Christian. Talk to *him* of the brotherhood of man, of loving his enemies, of doing good to them that hate him, of turning the other cheek, of the Kingdom of Heaven that is within him! He knows better.

ARTIFEX

He bargains with God (or the priest—it's all one) like another Abraham, and if he can swindle the saints he chuckles up his sleeve. The gods are powers to be placated or evaded, not missionaries of a way of life. The peasant had his way of life long before Jesus was born, and Jesus did very little to modify it, though he was a peasant himself.

The peasant is suspicious, but he has a right to be. Somehow, all through the ages, on one high-sounding pretext or another, he has always been robbed of what he produced, and left with barely enough or not enough to live on. The world rode on his shoulders, and called him a base-born hind for his pains. Often he is the descendant of serfs, and has their vices of lying and shiftiness. Why should a serf respect property or honour? He is avaricious, but his avarice is often a deep respect for the bread and wine which he alone knows cost so much in toil. He is ignorant—who teaches him? Superstitious—who enlightens him? Above all, he is intensely, ferociously conservative. And that is why he is so interesting—he has to some extent preserved a very ancient way of life. The very word "paganus," and its modern significance, shows his long obstinate resistance to the Church. His loyalty is of the old primitive kind. He cannot give it to anything so abstract as an institution, a state or an idea—only to the man who can understand, impress and inspire him. Directly he loses that loyalty, that ideal of service, he degenerates into a selfish trickster. He has always been the lowest of the low, ridden over by warrior, priest, merchant—all the tricksters of the towns. But take him for what he is, put him as low as you like, and then, from what his pig-headed conservatism has retained, see what his ancient masters did to civilize him, to make his life significant to him, to give him a sense of the mystery and grandeur of living. That is my cry—if the old world could give the base peasant so much, why need his masters give the enlightened voting industrial labourer so little? I don't mean in money, but in life. The answer is, that

ARTIFEX: SKETCHES AND IDEAS

having it not themselves, they cannot give it. And where are they to get it? Where the past got it, from Artifex? And where is he? In the hysterical cliques of London and Paris?

I must now recite to you a passage I have learned by heart from a book by one of the numerous worthy men who have undertaken to inform us of the surpassing benefits of modern science and industry. It runs:

"Everywhere in Europe and Asia where the peasant rules, sentimentalists delight to prate of its lovely local costumes and customs, its music and art. Everywhere, except for differences due to conditions of climate and natural resources, these costumes and art are practically the same, the industriously made lace, the bright buttons, the white linen, the red and black colourings, the tedious repetitive carving, the traditional music, the staid dancing, the plaintive and tragic song. It is essentially and indivisibly the same from Biscay and Brittany to China."

Now suppose this disparaging estimate were true —which it isn't—I would merely ask what are the costumes and customs, the music, the dancing, the song, the art of the industrial worker "from Biscay to China?" Are they even permitted, except as a spectacle or commodity which he passively endures, and which only exist to draw from him a little of his wages? This same author confesses elsewhere that the workers in Mr. Ford's factory—admittedly the most highly-paid in the world—are "only capable of the crudest recreations." Why? And that being so, has he any right to despise the little that the peasant can do, which is undoubtedly more than the industrial worker? The gentleman inspires me to rhymes:

> "*Let sentimentalists delight to prate*—
> I *am the prophet of the Perfect State.*
> *Blind, deafened, dumb with dear machinery,*
> *The world shall live in bliss—by reading Me!"*

ARTIFEX

The art of the uncontaminated peasant costs him nothing—he supports no impresarios, no Hollywood, no newspaper syndicates, no publisher and disinterested author, no esurient critic. Believe me, the great objection to peasant art is that *there's no money in it for any one;* and that is the sole reason why it is being persecuted out of existence. Not only does it make the peasant independent of the friends of humanity—which is wicked—but it keeps him independent of the factory owners, which is flat burglary. What's the good of the fellow if you can't sell him anything, if he and his wife make these ridiculous gaudy costumes for themselves, weave their own lace, make their own boots out of their own cowhides, make their own pots and plates, carve their own furniture from their own wood, and even build their own miserable huts? Never mind life—life's work for them and money for us—and never mind art—art's all rot anyway—*we've got to keep the machines going.*

And so from him that hath nothing even that which he hath is taken away.

As to the quality of peasant art as art, that is a matter of opinion. If you would accompany me to the Minho and Leiria, to the country round Gerona, to the Landes, to the Vorarlberg and Schwarzwald, to Calabria, the Abruzzi and Sicily, I think I could show you even yet specimens of this dying art which are far from contemptible. It is not true to say that the costumes are "the same," but it is true of the wretched machine-made reach-me-downs which take their place. Those drab and sordid and vulgar habiliments are indeed the same squalid disguise from Biscay to China—the women of the Leiria district look like queens. The women of Tiriolo are dressed like the wives of sixteenth-century Venetian grandees.

"Staid dancing"—have you ever seen a tarantella of Campania, a castanet dance of Andalusia, the round dances of north Portugal, a Russian boot dance, a Hungarian or Albanian dance? If they are staid, what is lively? Statistics or the tango? "Monotonous repetitive carving"—every district has its own style. "Plaintive and tragical song"—

> "*O Mari', O Mari',*
> *Una nott', una notte*
> *Con teeee!*"

And so one might go on. Our friend of humanity can't see anything there. And that's the trouble all the time—they just can't *see*. Senseless, in fact. You might as well ask a cocktail drinker's opinion of a fine claret.

But, come, this is poor talk for a decent wine-shop, and the caballeros will certainly think I am trying to sell you something big. I am—a gusto for living. Do I think anything will be altered by what I say? Frankly, I have mighty few hopes. I like to have my say, and I don't object too strenuously to paying my four and six in the pound, so long as I can say my say. I don't think it does much good; I'm sure it does no harm. And at any rate it gives me the illusion of living. In my opinion the friends of humanity are just as much up a blind alley as the theologians. There isn't any paradise, either here or hereafter; there isn't any solution of "the problem of life," because it isn't a problem. The only thing to do with life is to live it, put up with the tough breaks and enjoy the alleviations. To me the arts are among the highest of the alleviations—they are more than that, an indefinite prolonging and intensifying of life here and now. If they do not enrich experience of life both in artist and spectator, I see no point in them. But they do in a healthily balanced community. By killing out the arts from life and life from the arts, the modern world has impoverished its vitality.

ARTIFEX

Indeed, it may be said to be killing itself by cutting off one by one the very faculties and experiences which *are* life. Which may perhaps alleviate matters in the future. . . . But talking of alleviations, how about re-filling that decanter? Shall we drink to the memory of Artifex?

A Splinter of America

A Splinter of America

"AMERICA" now means the United States, but I am thinking of a splinter of tropical America broken from the mainland, almost hidden away in the southern ocean as far from New York as it is from Europe. It is the new-found land of Columbus and the first navigators, long before the Conquistadores and the northern pirates. Columbus never knew he had discovered another continent—two continents—but he found this island, and if he landed was the first European here.

Along which coast did he pass? From my window, if I look up from writing, I can see eight hundred feet below a vast expanse of empty grey-blue ocean. It has an almost primeval loneliness. Hour by hour and day by day its wavering colours change, sometimes clear blue under the blue sky, more often dappled or veiled with cloud shadows, sometimes hidden by the dark white-fringed curtain of a rain squall. But it is beautifully lonely. At most one sees the tiny white or dark speck of a fishing sail, hardly bigger than the white wave crests and almost lost among them. Once a small cargo steamer crawled past, and we all ran to look at this astonishing phenomenon. Today it is quite thronged—four sails scattered over square miles of ocean.

I please myself with the notion that the Spanish ships and

ARTIFEX: SKETCHES AND IDEAS

their Genoese admiral crossed this tract of sea I look on every day—it is the natural route with the north-east trade behind them, the windward side. The open space on which this house now stands was then a tangle of forest, yet it is a natural vantage-ground, and from here some of the Indians—if there were any—may have had a first glimpse of the white-winged monsters with their high poops and gorgeous banners, bringing them death and destruction in the name of universal love. A dangerous thing, that universal love.

The Mexicans had a tradition that long ago the Children of the Sun had come to them and taught them their arts and religion and social organization, and then had sailed away. But the Children of the Sun had said they would come back, and Montezuma thought the prophecy was fulfilled in Cortes. Only, the first Children of the Sun, according to the tradition, came from the *east*, across the Pacific. Who were they? The ethnologists have conflicting theories. A lovely name, Children of the Sun, but a grotesque and terrible irony when you think of what the Europeans have done to the Americas.

For a long time it was a fancy of mine that if I ever went to America I would go first to the America of Columbus, not to the mainland, but to the islands. The difficulty was to find an island which had not been cultivated out of all wildness and beauty. Barbados for instance. Poor Barbados, they have shaved off your wild shaggy beard, and left you sprouting an uninteresting stubble of not very valuable sugar cane. Having found my island with some difficulty I naturally feel I've done the right thing; I feel this is *the* way to discover the new world. The island is not virgin—rarissima avis—but there is enough left for me to imagine what it was.

Sky, sea, sun and moon are the same; the rest is strange. Even the stars seem unfamiliar—the tail of the Great Bear is lost in tree tops, and the Pole Star hangs a few degrees over the

A SPLINTER OF AMERICA

horizon. The very grass on my handkerchief of a lawn—the English *would* try to make lawns in the tropics!—the grass is not European grass, but broader-leafed, coarser, crisp under the feet. The earth is strange, especially to me who have never before crossed the Tropic of Cancer. A little thing stands for me as a symbol of the strangeness—the sensitive plant is a common weed, and I had only seen it tenderly nourished in greenhouses. Often I go out into the waste ground and touch one of the sensitive leaves, serrated like tiny palm trees, and watch it shiver and fold down its serrations and droop, followed by another leaf and another, till the whole plant is folded tight away. Marvellous! Sensitive plants, with their little fluffy pink flowers, growing wild! I can't get over the strangeness of it.

Here one soon drops into the natural earth and sun rhythm, waking with the crystalline dawn, fading to sleep in the early afternoon heat—Pan sleeps!—and waking up to another part-day of gold sunlight, flaring sunset and soft twilight, when we take our walks in the cool of the evening. Then supper, and our petrol lamps throwing long beams into the soft mysterious darkness outside, lit by stars above and swift flashing fireflies below, and noisily melodious with crickets and toads which tinkle like Spanish mules clinking and jingling their way over cobbles. But the very ease of adaptation destroys the sense of strangeness. Already it is fading, and I want to set down what little I can before it goes entirely.

The little town where one lands is unfortunately only too familiar in its lack of any distinction whatsoever. Here, as wherever modern people go, the first consideration is petty commerce; the second, petty convenience. That a township, even the merest village, can and should express much more than this has never occurred to them. Indeed they have nothing else to express. Their churches, like their religion, are mere

ARTIFEX: SKETCHES AND IDEAS

moral police stations. They are as devoid of aspiration as they are barren of beauty. Their public buildings breathe the ennui of officialdom. The summit of their architectural achievement is a splodge of fenced-in suburban villas with tedious flower plots and smooth dark roads—a concentration of ordinariness which suffocates the spirit. Amid the applause of scavengers and sanitary men they call it civilization. It is not what man has done here that is admirable, but what he has failed to destroy.

Yet—even as you are rowed ashore from the anchored ship, depressed by a panorama of red tin roofs among trees, you become aware of the strangeness. Something dark and mobile drops from the air with a sharp jab at the blue water. It dawns upon you that you have just seen a pelican, a wild pelican, gobbling a small fish. And yes, that group of large birds riding the small waves as tranquilly as geese on a pond are also pelicans—long-beaked dusky creatures, smaller than the white monsters of our parks and zoos. You look up and see another strange large bird gliding on the most elegant scimitar-shaped wings. He comes to rest on the dirty-looking sand under the seaward fringe of palms, and you see he is a kind of heron or crane, dove-blue and long-legged. What style! He is like a bird on a fine Chinese lacquer screen....

Up here, eight miles from "civilization," we are still not out of the zone of improvement, but it is wild and strange enough for the ignorant and not too intrepid traveller. Round here the island is not more than demi-vierge, not so much primeval as going a little derelict—slump in the cocoa and margarine world. Well, I for one shall do nothing to stop the rot. Among the many interesting things I look out on from my verandahs is a large patch—several acres—of trees. They are not virgin forest, but the forest returning. I believe they are temporarily

A SPLINTER OF AMERICA

mine—I'm not sure of the boundaries of this estate, but I think they must be. If they were "mine"—as if one could really own such grand and mysterious things as great trees!—how I should cherish them, how jealously guard that sanctuary from the civilizing jerry-builder. I should be tempted to imitate Voltaire when he built a church, and put up an inscription: "Dis consecravit Aldington, Trespassers will be shot."

Not everything up here is unfamiliar. An oleander is putting out its delicate pink blossoms, which look very modest beside the gorgeous splendours of hibiscus, poinsettia and bougainvillea. Oleanders always make me think of Sirmione, where a long line of them drops—or used to drop, for the world is being fast improved out of such sentimentalities—little flotillas of pink petals on the sulphurous blue water of Lake Garda. Bougainvillea brings back the south of France, only here they are not all that mauve purple. I have a superb scarlet one, and regret I haven't also one of the beautiful salmon pink variety which grow so superbly in this climate. The poinsettias are a disappointment, not to be compared with those of Portugal—but then Portugal is the land of flowers. Where I do score is with hibiscus—also not a native, by the way. I have heard hibiscus disparaged as "gaudy," but my own prayer would be: O gods, give me more such gaudiness. It was over hibiscus I saw my first green and gold flashing humming-bird, with his loud purring wings, uttering little mouse-like squeaks as he poked into flowers bigger than himself.

Up here we should have a pageant of hibiscus if an idiot black hadn't checked their growth by slashing them level. And hibiscus blossoms from its topmost shoots. If you want the flowers you must let them straggle. But they are struggling out, for everything grows swiftly—there is no check of cold day or night. I had no idea there were so many varieties, from pure scarlet through every tone of paler red and orange to

ARTIFEX: SKETCHES AND IDEAS

cream yellow and pure white. Some are checkered white and red or cream yellow and red—I can't remember them all. There are even double ones, like ragged pink roses. But at this point I grow uncertain. I recognize the blue plumbago, but what is this creeper with a flower like a white clematis, but assuredly not a clematis? What is this ground-dweller, which at evening unfolds a large pure white trumpet which has withered by morning? What are these other, rather insignificant, flowering shrubs, the one with the blue and white bugle, another with clusters of orange red tubes?

Yet neither the garden nor the woods are really flowery. The tropic exuberance seems to run to root, stem and leaf. In this contest of vegetation I suppose any plant or tree is lucky if it can dodge out a few flowers at an unexpected moment, rather as poets timidly put forth their works in between the publishing seasons. Yet one mustn't judge hastily. These apparently flowerless and penurious trees can become gorgeous in a night. When we arrived the immortelles filled the woods with huge splashes of flamy orange flowers which grow in freesia-like crests from the bare boughs. They are nearly all gone now. A week ago a liana abruptly produced a thick tracery of ragged purple flowers on the green wall of trees. One evening we found an insignificant shrub covered thick with jasmin-like (but scentless) white stars. The almost imperceptible buds of one evening were the full flowers of the next.

But already I am wandering out along the plantation tracks when I meant first to speak of what can be seen from the garden and verandahs. Even among the flowers I have forgotten the sickly-scented tuberoses, the ragged pink begonias—reminiscent of suburbs—and a large yellow flower like a brighter and stronger night-lily. Upon the whole, it is not such a bad display considering that this is the middle of the unflowery dry season.

A SPLINTER OF AMERICA

At the south end of one verandah is a huge tree which has the strange attraction of being at once an aërial garden and a free aviary. It is a Saman—like a huge locust or acacia, though the flower is different. A fortnight ago it was shedding its old leaves like rain, and already it is a flutter of new greenery. The vast trunk and lower boughs are covered with drooping moss and little fern-like plants, now brown and shrivelled for lack of moisture. Among these are other strange parasites, one like a creeping cactus, another like an enormous cos lettuce, others like a small laurel. There is one parasite which must live on air, for it perches itself on telegraph wires which can't be particularly nourishing. Another looks like a small not very interesting aloe, and then shoots up a long branched red stalk dangling prickly big wheat ears, green touched with white and blue. These parasites are more luxurious in the damper woods, but I haven't yet got over the strangeness of looking straight out on a tree which grows a dozen species of plants on itself.

This tree is a hunting-ground for the many tropical birds which are comparatively unafraid of humans. In one way the strangest bird that comes is a little thing that looks exactly like a willow wren and sings rather like one. I could scarcely believe my eyes and ears when I first saw and heard him—what is this little cockney doing here? More appropriate are the blue birds, which flit about like bits of sky, light blue below, dark blue above. The Jamaica woodpecker, with his red crest and white-laced wings, comes and taps loudly and unconcernedly. He is followed by a small dusky black bird no bigger than a robin, which shows a flash of dazzling white as it lifts its wings.

The proprietor of the tree is a tiny but irascible and incredibly courageous green humming-bird, which fearlessly attacks any intruder forty times its size. There are the weird tick birds, black as a crow, shaped like a magpie, with short heavy bills—they hang about donkeys and cows for their ticks and amaze you by uttering a note like a curlew. Well, they are

ARTIFEX: SKETCHES AND IDEAS

so afraid of the humming-bird they daren't come near the tree. He doesn't seem to mind the smaller birds—the blue birds, the woodpeckers, the wrens, the mocking-bird, the small yellow-and-blue birds and many others—but anything big enrages him. The other day a big yellow-tail dared to come and sit on the tree. These are the birds which build the hanging nests from the tips of high branches where they swing in the wind like jelly-bags made of hay—I know one tree which has sixteen of these unsightly objects on it. The birds are black and yellow with heavy white beaks and are great fruit-eaters—I see they've been at the pawpaws this morning. Eccentric birds in their noises as well as in their nesting—a favourite trick of theirs is to yell to attract attention, stand on their heads, ingeniously imitate the creaking of bamboos in the wind and say: Popocatapetl.

The humming-bird was furious at the sight of this clowning creature sitting creaking on his tree. I could see him perched on a distant twig trepidant with rage, shaking his wings and waving his tiny conductor's baton of a beak as if he were conducting the Walkyrie. In between the yellow-tail's sinister creaking I could faintly hear his mousey squeals of fury. Suddenly the humming-bird shot up from his twig, poised, and flung himself like a fiery bullet, zum! just a fraction over the other bird's head, turned and fired himself back again, zum! Back and forth he went, zum! zum! and each time the yellow-tail ducked ignominiously. Up and down went the flashing whirring little projectile, zum! zum! a tiny glistening Perseus, courageous as they make them, until at last he drove the monster yellow-tail off and pursued him with lilliputian shrieks of anger. And people talk of "the gentle humming-bird!" Iridescent little devils they are. . . .

The ground slopes away from the house in all but one direction, and on either side are steepish but not very profound

A SPLINTER OF AMERICA

valleys. Here the fruit trees are planted. Talk of Milton's "burnished globes"—not very good for ripe fruits really, too much like polished lamps. But here indeed is an Eden of fruit: the most orangey orange-coloured tangerines I ever saw bending the boughs with their weight of "globes" in spite of our daily lightening; large smooth yellow grapefruit sweet as tangerines, and yellow-green shaddocks which are like double-sized grapefruit but not so good; lemons which look like oranges, and oranges which are sometimes nearly as green as lemons but sweeter even than those of Sicily; sapodillas which look like small clean potatoes and have hard black stones in them and taste a little perverse and sinful—some people like them; pawpaws which grow like small ugly melons on a tree stem and of which you only eat the inner rind; small aromatic limes which are such a lovely green when you cut them; and a small forest of bananas, their vast thin leaves torn into shreds by the trade-wind so that they might almost be palm leaves. And there are eight or ten dark massive mango trees not in fruit at this time of year.

Perhaps I have been over-particular and tedious in this catalogue of my island foreground. You must imagine it arched over by a vast ever-changing sky, bounded by wooded hills, falling away gracefully past a screen of colossal feathery bamboos to the low land by the sea where the last lines of palms stand out clear against the blue water. My experience has showed me that the foreground of one's life is the more important. Among the millions of people in a great city one's friends outweigh all the others in value, though there is always the thought that the anonymous background *may* include the very people for whom one is yearning. We must cultivate hope. One of the most beautiful coasts in Europe is that between Monte Carlo and Vintimiglia, a superb background of sea and mountain. Unluckily the foreground is a horror, a noisy prison from which there is no escape. By turning the landscape into a means of livelihood men have destroyed its life—an intelligent process going on all over the world.

This foreground of brilliant flowers, strange trees, graceful or amusing birds, is at present important in my life. I shouldn't care to live in the community near Government House, though it might provide conveniences I don't want and company with which I cheerfully dispense. I have but to step to the other end of the verandah and there I shall find that huge old tree—"art thou there, truepenny?"—with his queer cargo of parasites and his floating population of bright-hued birds. Perhaps because most of these forms of vivid life are so strange to me I feel more than ever the mysteriousness of these beings which are so different from me and yet connected with me. I find myself pondering the eternal What? How? Why? I lose myself in faint intuitions and vague speculations.

Man is the measure of all things in the sense that he cannot go beyond his capacity in knowing and feeling. Even if everything seemed to be known and experienced, still there must always be the doubt, always the possibility of vast or little mysteries entirely beyond the registering power of the human instrument. This is true also of common known things. I cannot possibly know what it really is to be a tree or a bird. My consciousness may be superior—it is flattering to think so—but it doesn't include theirs. The essence of their life and being is for ever mysterious. Analysis burkes the question, and vivisection is only maiming.

Is it unfair to proud man to say that ultimately he has only invented two, equally unsatisfactory, answers to the What? How? Why? Providence and Chance, religion and science, Egypt and Greece—though I believe the word Providence is Plato's. But the theory of Providence leads to the burdensome monstrosity of theology and such absurd propositions as that all "lower life" was made for man's use—much use a

A SPLINTER OF AMERICA

humming-bird is to me! The trouble with Providence is that it doesn't provide. The theory that man can do as he likes with all forms of "lower" life, that it is heretical to suppose he has any duties there, is a formula for making deserts—but it is a logical development of the Providence theory. Unluckily when man makes a desert, as he has contrived to do in some parts of the earth, Providence does nothing about it. The desert remains, and the lord of creation fades out of the picture.

The theory that things just happened, that an accidentally-formed universe necessarily is a sort of machine, that all living things are little machines "behaving"—that theory seems equally absurd and is unfortunately equally flattering to the destructive instincts of mankind. Doubtless the layman misunderstands science as chronically as he has misunderstood religion. But is it scientific to ignore the fact that man is a creature with a genius for misunderstanding or perverting what he understands? Those leaders of thought admirably described by the French as "strugforlifers" have represented life as a perpetual war between "Man" and "Nature." Is it? Are we really at war with our environment? It seems to be merely another formula for making deserts and Hitlers.

Of course I have over-simplified and thus distorted both ideas, but I refuse to involve myself in the subtleties of theological dialectic and scientific metaphysics. I have nothing to say to the modern scientist-theologians who assert God with their eyebrows and deny Him with their elbows. If they really believe in God they can't get away from Providence. An Epicurean God who spends eternity in thinking "How comfortable I am," won't do; neither will a metaphysical God occupied with the thought "How clever I am." I am concerned with the practical results of these two theories, and it seems to me the end of both is the same—destruction and desert-making. It doesn't matter whether you destroy life by believing that God says you may and that He will provide, or whether

ARTIFEX: SKETCHES AND IDEAS

you do it by a series of Pyrrhic triumphs over "Nature" and swarm humanity into indigence.

It seems to me there might be another attitude to life, based on an acceptance of life's mystery and on reverence for its many forms, a more modest conception of man's place in nature, and abhorrence of every kind of greed and destruction. One seems to get glimpses of it in the more ancient civilizations, in the lives of some men, in some poets and even in a few philosophers. I think I might be able to put up something of a case for it—but to what end? The world is far too populous and far too chaotic for any effective influence even of a great conception greatly expressed. And I am not so conceited as to think I could achieve that. The most one can do is to follow one's own daimon as far as the swarming masses and their perplexed officials will allow one, and that unfortunately isn't very far. The part of self-appointed saviour of society has become odious and ridiculous. Perhaps there is nothing to be saved. In any case "society" doesn't care a hoot what I may think or say, so why bother? Let me save myself before I presume to save others.

Certainly from the vantage-point of this lonely island it looks as if humanity were far gone in the throes of self-destruction, either through fratricidal wars or weariness of the sweet earth through colossal rabbit warrens of people or by reducing existence to terms of such imbecility that life will fail from sheer ennui. I say "it looks"; it may not be so at all; it may be that the radio, the airplane, the fenced-in suburb, the potted science and the potty newspaper, turning to the right by numbers and living out of tins, are what you really want and will make you happy. It may be that the poison gas, if and when it comes, will translate you, like Bottom the weaver, to the lap of Titania. I don't know. But I do know I can't do anything about it—and so I'll (without Mr. Browning's "heigh-ho") go look at my hibiscus. . . .

A SPLINTER OF AMERICA

After this bout of speculation, which the judicious reader may skip, let me come back to my splinter of America. But when it is a question of trying to talk about the things I see on my walks here I become concerned for my ignorance. Really I don't even know the names of half the things I see. I wish I had Squire Waterton for a neighbour; how gladly I would promise not to offend the old gentleman's religious scruples if he would promise to give me his knowledge. It would be worth a Mass or two. But there is no Waterton, and I must console myself with the thought that my ignorance is a condition of the strangeness I find so attractive. In fact, ignorance is a condition of this piece of writing. Unless the reader is a little more ignorant even than I am, I can't see it being much fun for him. And if he knows the tropics, has lived in them for years, his only fun will be seeing my mistakes. . . .

Like other distinguished people, we take our walks in the cool of the evening. It is still fairly hot about four, but reasonably so, and there are well over two hours of sunlight left. By seven it is quite dark. The sunsets are often vivid in colour, but brief and nothing exceptional; I have seen far more gorgeous displays over the marshes of Sandwich. Doubtless the weather is unprecedented within the memory of the oldest inhabitant—it always is.

The track—I can scarcely call it a drive—winds downhill to the main road, which itself is only a lane, covered with dry leaves and bamboo leaves, and overgrown with grass and weeds. The hibiscus and bougainvillea continue for some way, then a high bank with blossoming saplings of locust and a queer cactus-looking plant on the right, and a plantation of bananas, limes and coconuts on the left. Where the track twists over a dried-up streamlet I can look across at a piece of land which is either lying fallow or reverting to bush, whichever you choose. Already it is waist-deep in burrs and thorns and the unpleasant mongrel-looking weeds which seem to flourish wherever a natural growth has been destroyed. For unknown thousands of years it was forest, in its own way a perfect expression of mysterious life, until economic man attacked it with fire and axe, with the useless and uncomely result I now behold. Perhaps in a few decades it might become forest again. But the deeds of economic man are certainly marvellous and make me think of a saying in one of Mr. Shaw's plays: "Them as was with 'er when she died would 'ave done 'er in for sixpence." What was done in there was a bit of primeval America, and what it produces now isn't worth sixpence.

Where the track meets the road a narrow gorge suddenly drops away into a wide wooded valley, and the stream, brown with leaf mould, falls in a thin cascade which is no doubt a cataract in the rainy season. Downhill the road winds in a corniche to a village and eventually to the sea. In either direction one passes plantations of closely-set cocoa trees, with their curious green or reddish or purplish gourd-pods strangely sticking from the trunk or boughs. But the most obvious feature of this mountain stream is undoubtedly the immense and beautiful clumps of bamboo. Put from your mind memories of flimsy bamboo furniture and of the little clumps of wild canes in south Europe. These, though not exactly masts for some great ammiral, are as thick and tall as the masts of a yacht. They feather out gracefully at the tips and, bowing to each other in the wind, form exquisite moving arches overhead. The ungainly rubber trees which grow among them are a curious contrast with their ugly knobbed boughs and leaves lopping down like rabbits' ears. And again there is the further contrast of the wild palms, so erect and graceful, with their crowns of huge fluttering leaves ten or fifteen feet long.

The road winds on mostly upward and mostly through cocoa plantations, passing only two houses, for close on a couple of miles, until it suddenly descends on to the stream and

A SPLINTER OF AMERICA

skirts what seems to my ignorant eyes a strip of primeval forest. At any rate there is a vast tangle of enormous tropical trees and palms bound together with lianas—looking in fact extremely like the engravings of American forests in the books of one's boyhood. I haven't attempted to enter; it couldn't be done without a cutlass to cut a way through, and one doesn't want to be found playing the part of an intrepid explorer in the shrubbery of a tropical gentleman's estate. Only in this case the shrubbery is eighty to a hundred feet high, and as one peers into its solemn shadows pillared with great trunks the cathedrals of Europe seem almost trivial. Yet whatever gods may inhabit that solitude do not seem bloodthirsty or hostile. I am conscious of none of that "uneasiness of mind" which I have read is created by the spectacle of the "strugforlife" of tropical vegetation. A peaceful exuberance—and its dark silence is broken only by some insect which makes a noise like a shrill rattle, and is certainly not a rattle-snake. The recesses of the Amazon valley are doubtless more formidable and dangerous.

Yet I shall not soon forget this first glimpse of wild forest. In Europe most of our woods have been planted and tended by man and are usually of one or two kinds of trees—oak woods or beech woods. Here there were so many different kinds of trees one gave up in despair trying to notice differences of leaf, trunk and colour, and relapsed into a general impression of trees, lianas and undergrowth. From a human point of view, which is always proposing illusory aims and ends, it seems an almost pointless demonstration of vital energy. These trees have no aim except to be, and trees have existed there for uncountable centuries. Yet this fragment of primeval forest creates a feeling of religious awe. Here one touches a mystery. Economic man can come along and cut it down; scientific man can explain it away with specious theories; tourist man can run by it in a car. But, there are more things in heaven and earth, Horatio. Yet there is nothing to "under-

ARTIFEX: SKETCHES AND IDEAS

stand." There is "only" something mysterious and lovely, like genius and beauty in men and women, to which one responds. The forest gave me something which will not appear in my pass-book and is not in the text-books. I was not even inspired to cut it down, and substitute healthy economic crops.

At this season of the year this is a flowerless land. When I think of what Portugal is now and what France will be in a few weeks I am almost tempted to regret Europe. The roadside, which should ideally be studded with flowers, is an undistinguished tangle of greenery. On the trees are the strange red and green "flowers" of spiky parasites. There is an Aroid, with leaves like harts-tongue nourished on the food of the gods—eight feet long—and red angular cups stiff on a stiff stem. There are horn-shaped dark scarlet blossoms on a little shrub, almost invisible in so much green. In a nook where one would expect primroses or cyclamen in Italy a solitary pineapple astonishingly announces itself. Across the stream is one single specimen of a remarkable white flower, like a pale melancholy mop upside down. The gorgeous immortelle flowers are over, and the white jasmin-like shrub referred to before flowered only for five days. Quickly come and quickly go seems to be the rule. Only yesterday a dull shrub had suddenly erupted into a gorgeous scarlet flower. Tomorrow it may be gone.

There are few insects. In the silence a single huge black bumble-bee around the locust flowers hums like an airplane. An insignificant and debilitated white and black butterfly flickers languidly in the lanes. Elsewhere one comes on dark Hairstreaks and the tiniest Blue ever imagined. The great tropical butterflies are rare. In the twilight one evening a bat flew nearly in my face—but no, it was a huge grey and blue moth, eyed like a peacock. There is a Vanessa, like a cross between a Red Admiral and a Tortoiseshell; a gorgeous black and red beauty outside my limited knowledge; a superb Apollo;

A SPLINTER OF AMERICA

a Camberwell Beauty who has strayed far from Camberwell and changed a little in doing so. Common Sulphurs flicker across the garden. But one of these exotic beauties is an event on a walk. It must be winter for the butterflies.

Yesterday we picked up the shimmering blue wing of a Morpho. The birds must keep them rare as they keep down other insects. Every step of the way one feels the presence of the birds flitting and calling from their hiding places in the trees. Some are bold and care nothing for the enemy man; others very shy. Every morning and evening I hear the rapid coc-o-ree-co, coc-o-ree-co, of the wild pheasants—I have never yet seen one. There are said to be parrots—none vouchsafe themselves. But one hears the birds on all sides. Now it is the swift tap-tap-tap-tap of woodpeckers, now the sentimental cooing of wild doves, the *tortole*, now the antic shrieks of the yellow-tail. Some one is tormenting a puppy and making it squeal abjectly. Very odd—half a dozen people are making half a dozen puppies squeal. Then suddenly I catch sight of a woodpecker crouched against the trunk of a cocoa tree—he is the squealing puppy! A voice over my head says "Popo-catapetl"—it is only a trick of the yellow-tail. The air purrs behind me, mysterious in the silence—a peacock green, white streaked humming-bird. In a flash of bronze green he is gone.

Suddenly we are silent, and then move slowly forward. On the branch of a cocoa tree, only a few yards away, a pair of the King of the Woods sit in silent motionless dignity. American-fierce as an Aztec, proud as Montezuma, they sit aloof and indifferent in their gorgeous cloaks—rippling, red-sunset-hue chests, blue-green-gold iridescent back and wings, vivid blue crest, twin blue tail plumes, part naked and ending in a tiny blue battledore. King and Queen are nearly always together, and almost exactly alike. No question here of the male dazzling the humble female with his fine feathers—she is exactly as fine as he is. No utility in such a madrigal of colour—

ARTIFEX: SKETCHES AND IDEAS

it doesn't hide him and he is a succulent morsel for the eagles. There he sits, indifferent, with his heavy black bill, another Montezuma, perfect in himself, superb. Shoot him? As much a senseless sacrilege as to shoot the Sun, whose child he is. Leave him to his perfection and be glad for him.

The King has a small cousin I call the Prince—his real name is Jacamar—similar in colouring, except that he has tried the effect of tying on a small white bib, which I think an error in taste. He hasn't the Amerindian dignity of his monarch, but wallows in dust baths or perches alert, his long thin black beak sharp as a dagger, waiting for insects. Swoop, flutter, turn, swoop back—he has caught something I have not been quick enough to notice, but I see him voluptuously swallowing. A succulent wild bee no doubt. The King never speaks to him, never looks at him—probably scorns his plagiarized colours and the slight error of that white bib. I am not so censorious, I am grateful for the Prince too. He knew perfection when he saw it. . . .

It is strange to wake in the night and catch a glimpse of unfamiliar stars through the open window and think: I am in America, the other side of the world. I have travelled so many thousands of miles in many countries, yet scarcely crossed the limits of the Roman Empire. Now I am in this little splinter of the vast American world which the Romans never dreamed of, for all the legends of Atlantis. And it is a *new* world. There is a strange lightness about it, a release as if one's spirit had slipped a burden. The landscape is not weighed down with the memory of dead generations, the air is not thick with ghosts. I expected such oppressive hostile gods, and it is all so new, almost genial, if a little reserved. I find nothing sinister—on the contrary, this feeling of lightness and freshness, this release from the maddening oppression of Europe.

Letters and newspapers come from time to time, a neighbour

A SPLINTER OF AMERICA

drops in with hair-raising news of Europe. I read and I listen, but care no longer. Really Europe doesn't seem to matter here, and I feel as if at long last I had escaped from a vast congress of bad-tempered neurotics. Having confused all issues, complicated all aims beyond the power of unravelling, slaughtered all simplicity and made life an extremely disagreeable and tedious farce, the European nations stand bellowing vulgar threats and insults at each other, while their clever men feverishly prepare their mutual destruction. Well, if they must destroy themselves, they must. Perhaps better that than to go on as they are, like demented dogs going round faster and faster in pursuit of their own tails. Is it peace or war? Here, at any rate, it is peace.

Abel

Abel

ABEL isn't his real name. Like most negroes his mother or his godparents had a passion for the grandiose in names—as if, like medieval philosophers, they believe the name to be the reality—and called him after an archangel and a Roman Emperor. So that to rename him merely after a patriarch is rather a come-down. But for the present let him be called Abel.

I like Abel very much. At the moment he is "head boy" of my very small household of coloured servants—"de butler" as he prefers to call himself, though that again is far too grandiose. To me he is something of a problem. I don't mean in the ordinary and tiresome sense that servants are "a problem"— indeed I think Abel is about the best servant I ever had, though I have been extremely lucky as a rule in servants. The problem —if that is the word—arises from the fact that in this American Island I am served by a descendant of Africans. It strikes me as strange that in an Island which was inhabited by Arawaks or Caribs (I forget which) when Columbus discovered it, I, a white man from North Europe, should be served by this dark man from another continent. A strange, tragical, sordid drama of history went to make possible our very ordinary relation.

The quality of the service Abel gives is what interests me,

for in elegance or knowledge of how things are done in the middle classes he would be hopelessly beaten by any moderately trained Englishman. Yet I greatly prefer his service to that of the most perfectly English butler imaginable. Something of the kind I have come across before in remote parts of Austria and Italy, where the old peasant tradition of loyalty and service to an imaginary better class still exists. I say "imaginary" because the supposed "better" class is now only too frequently inferior in real virtue to the peasant. But in remote places the peasant still clings to the tradition that there is something mystically great and powerful and beautiful about "the masters," and wants to serve them, enjoys doing it, feels somehow inspired and deeply satisfied by doing so.

It is the same with Abel. Only with him the mystery of service is still quite pure, there is in him not the shadow of doubt that in serving me he is serving something far greater and more wonderful than himself. I say "something" and not "somebody" intentionally, for though I flatter myself that he is beginning to be attached to me personally, what he really serves is his idea of me. To him—strange irony of circumstance!—I am a representative of the mysterious white race, children of the gods, the rulers, lords of a mighty empire. And far more for Abel's sake than for the Empire's I find I do my best not to let the Empire down, or rather his almost religious idea of it.

Don't run away with the idea that Abel is servile or that I like servility. I hate servility, particularly the fawning insolent servility of European servants—in hotels and restaurants—who serve only for money and do it with malevolent grudging. Abel isn't a bit servile. He doesn't feel the slightest need to assert his rights as a man, because he is absolutely certain that I shall not infringe them. Again I say it is not so much the personal me he serves. We are both part of an order in which it is my destiny to command and his to obey. He trusts implicitly

ABEL

that my command and his obedience are serving some valuable end—heaven knows what, not the stock market I trust. True I pay him wages, but they are insignificant—I am almost ashamed, they are so little. At least I was, until the true nature of our relationship dawned on me. Then I saw that while I take from him I always give to him. I give him almost the most valuable intangible thing one can give another—a complete mystical faith that he is serving something higher than himself. Naturally I see the irony of it, but it is a grave irony. Nor is it so unserviceable. At last I feel the force of noblesse oblige. I feel entirely under an obligation not to let Abel down. Fortunately my self-love informs me that I'm quite as good as any whites Abel is likely to have known, if not a bit better. Otherwise I might get a little restive.

It is very interesting to observe Abel when some matter of household service brings him into my part of the bungalow. I mustn't stare at him—if I do, he looks at me quickly to know what he is doing wrong. I must go on with what I'm doing, and observe him occultly, in glances which are swifter than his rhythm. That is another thing I like about Abel—his life rhythm is not exactly slow or deliberate, but it is totally unflurried, unconscious; it is like a natural earth rhythm, whereas mine is the impatient almost mechanically swift rhythm of the self-conscious white. I see the secret of his perfect tranquillity —he has for the time being put the responsibility of his life on me. I am the responsible one in this queer unexpected partnership. If there is any worrying to be done, I'm the one to do it, not Abel. He's perfectly confident that I shall worry out right in the end.

So when Abel comes into my rooms he makes me think of Agag, for he treads delicately. Not that he comes in awkwardly, he's as supple and balanced as a cat, but he comes in reverently, with real reverence, as if into the presence of a son of the gods. Sometimes he comes in so silently I don't hear him, and am startled to find his dark face in the room. "Ah'm sorry to disturb you, Master, but . . ." It is a matter of importance. An old coloured woman has brought some sweet potatoes and yams, and wants threepence instead of a lawful tuppence—my authority must be exerted; or "de yard boy" is going down to the village on the daily errand, and orders must be given. And having received the answer of the mysterious one, Abel goes out, cat-like, silent, fully satisfied.

A ceremony which daily delights me is to see Abel laying the tea things. We have tea in the long gallery instead of in the dining-room, so I can watch him unobserved from my writing nook at the far end. As he puts things on the table, he stands far, far away, as from a sacred place, and leans right forward from his supple loins. He evidently gets the deepest satisfaction from this holy ceremonial. And he has the most delicate sure way of touching objects and of laying them down—I think all the dark races have. He never drops or breaks anything. His whole attention is concentrated on what he is doing—he never seems to be wool-gathering or thinking vaguely of half a dozen things at once, as we do. He sets down a cup and saucer as if he were laying down a flower, not hesitatingly or slap-dash, but—there. Nothing ever has to be moved or rearranged. He has a sensitive awareness of objects which makes me happy to see. There must be centuries upon centuries of racial culture behind him—not our intellectual culture, but something quite different, as mysterious to me as my culture is to him. When I see that beautiful sensitiveness in Abel, and think of the brutality of the white slave-traders. . . .

They tell me Abel is an exception, that I'm very fortunate to have him, that most of "them" are cheats and thieves and liars. No doubt, but what should one expect of recently emancipated slaves? If you do that great wrong to people, you can't expect their immediate descendants to have the virtues of responsibility. But Abel wasn't born in this island.

ABEL

"He comes from X Island," I was told. "It's a queer place, hardly any colour bar. All the natives are a better type."

Immediately I am interested.

"Why? How do you explain it?"

"Oh, I dunno. Probably they have more money and go away for their education."

Je donne ma langue aux chats, as Madame de Sévigné used to say when exasperated. Here I am told of a certain place where there is "hardly any colour bar" and the people are of a good type. And the explanation is that they go for their education to places where the coloured people are admittedly of a lower type—so how in the name of logic could that "improve" the X islanders? But the fact of superiority in a certain island—if true—is certainly interesting. Could it be that the negroes were originally of a finer African race? This seems impossible when you think of the mix-up of tribes snatched away in the hazard of raids—black chiefs and commoners and their slaves of all sorts of districts all mixed up. And is the "hardly any colour bar" a cause or an effect? I mean are the people better because there is very little colour prejudice or vice versa? But you might as well ask the rocks about such things as ask the English "governing class"—let's turn on the wireless and have a game of bridge.

But, though I admire and feel touched by Abel's ideal of service—or what I imagine it to be—I have to admit that it makes me feel a humbug. It is all very well to talk about the principle of aristocracy, that the less should serve the greater, that the "common man" should find his happiness, his sanction for life, in the faith that he is serving something finer than himself even if he doesn't understand it. The trouble is that there are no real aristocrats today, there is only money. The Empire itself is merely a gigantic money-making concern—which, like Dogberry, has had losses, and will have more. It has its hired bravi and its hired managers, some—perhaps many—of whom

ARTIFEX: SKETCHES AND IDEAS

still sincerely believe in a mystical something about the Empire which is greater than money. But listen to them, let them talk—it is all cant, they have no ideal except the fallacious one of their own superiority to everything and everyone. Whom the gods wish to destroy . . . Even though they themselves don't make money, they are none the less the servants of the money-making concern. They are not patiently spreading a higher civilization—they haven't one to spread. The genuine civilizing elements in English life are impotent for good, patronized and paid a little if they fundamentally play up to the money-making idea, crushed if they genuinely oppose it.

So I think that Abel gives his rather beautiful selfless devotion to a sham. That is the difficulty with all aristocracies, they all tend to become a sham. They may start with or they may acquire a genuine indisputable superiority, but they have never learned how to keep it. Humanity has never yet learned to breed true a class of genuinely superior men and women. It can only breed a "manner," an outward appearance of superiority, as the English do now. But when you get a sham aristocracy, some inferior power takes its place—and today that is money. Even the new bludgeon and knuckle-duster aristocracies of the Continent are at the service of the money-making idea. And so it is in England—in the midst of our chaos of half-baked democracy and half-baked aristocracy, the real power is that of money. If you believe that England is still genuinely an aristocracy, ask yourself what fate is more piteous and humiliating than that of a penniless peer of the realm. And if you believe it is a genuine democracy, consider the fate of the free and equal citizen on the dole. So it's money first and money last and money all the time, and if you haven't got money you might as well go and hang yourself. Only—and it is a big only—service to the money idea somehow leaves men profoundly dissatisfied and restive, makes them feel empty and cheated. So that sooner or later the money States must and will

ABEL

collapse. Or, at least, so I think—perhaps I am wrong. . . .

Now if the word of the Lord came unto me, saying: "Where is Abel thy brother?" I should have to answer: "O Lord, Thou knowest, he is in my kitchen." But if the Lord went on and said: "Why is he in thy kitchen when I, even I, appointed him to dwell in his own tent in another land, even the land of Ethiopia?"—if the Lord said that I shouldn't know how to answer. If I felt cheeky I might say: "Well, why didn't You see that he stayed there?" Or if I felt inclined to accept a responsibility which is only mine by inheritance—an inheritance I repudiate—I should say, "O Lord, we have sinned—but it's no good sending Abel back to the tents of Ethiopia, he would hate it." And if the Lord, growing more familiar and reasonable said: "What do you intend to do about it?" I should grow argumentative and say: "Now, look here, Lord, if You are really the Master of the world, the responsibility is on You; if not, I don't intend to allow You to put on me a responsibility that is not mine. I personally am *not* Abel's keeper," so that would be that—but it wouldn't alter the fact that my remote ancestors did a great wrong to Abel's remote ancestors. If Abel's ancestors had wanted to serve them, well and good; but it was barbarous and wrong to compel them. . . .

The history of the relations between the Europeans and other peoples in the Americas makes unhappy reading. The story has not ended yet, not by any means. And when one tries to sum it up to date there seems little to be said except that ignorant and blundering sentimentality has tried to correct the errors—not to use a harsher term—of ignorant and blundering cruelty and greed. Perhaps the best thing that was done was the Jesuit State of Paraguay, and the enlightened M. de Voltaire made a gross error when he rejoiced in its overthrow. But one doesn't know—history is like a Brocken spectre, magnifying the prejudices of historians.

When the Spaniards first discovered the outlying isles of

ARTIFEX: SKETCHES AND IDEAS

their new-found land, they reported the existence of two nations, the Caribs and the Arawaks. The Spaniards say that these nations were at war, that the Caribs were man-eaters and made raids upon the Arawaks to supply their unholy appetites. According to them the Caribs were monsters of ferocity and beastliness. The Arawaks on the other hand were almost too good to be true—gentle, sweet-natured children of nature who needed only conversion to the True Faith to become angels straight away. Then we learn that the Caribs didn't like the Spaniards intruding on their lands and received them with showers of arrows and spears; whereas the Arawaks made the strangers welcome, gave them food and listened with awed amazement to their theologians.

These early explorers seem to have lived in a remarkable state of mental confusion. They seem quite incapable of distinguishing between myth and fact, between what they saw and what they thought they ought to see. They misreport true things, overlook the obvious and invent absurdities. They invented Patagonian giants, men with umbrella feet, Anthropophagoi that do bear their heads between their shoulders; their draughtsmen gave the Indians classical profiles and costumes, and made an alligator look like a preposterous cross between a hog and a bear. And as nobody could contradict, they were free to invent anything—particularly to justify their own excesses. They may quite well have invented the cannibalism of the Caribs and the angelic natures of the Arawaks, only because they were respectively hostile and friendly.

But whatever sort of people the Arawaks and Caribs were, they were destined by their Christian converters to the same fate—subjugation and slavery. But here, in the very beginning, the Spaniards came up against the stupid obstinacy of the heathen. The Caribs were such pestilentially good fighters that it was very difficult to enslave them; in fact small pockets of Caribs maintained their independence for a very long time.

Oddly enough, more recent investigators of the remnants of Caribs report with unfeigned surprise that they are quite gentle and know nothing about cannibalism.

At first the Arawaks out of pure good-nature did what the Spaniards told them—hospitably entertained them, lent them their women, gave them gold or pearls in exchange for any old trash, and did their chores. Then one day the Arawaks discovered that the great idea behind Christianity is that they should go on doing this for ever. They rebelled; whereupon they were hunted like wild beasts, shot, tortured, beaten, chained—enslaved in fact. But though the Arawaks were too angelic to be able to resist gunpowder they were evidently a proud people. They solved the problem in a way most displeasing to the Spaniards—they actually committed race suicide, like the Carthaginians. They dashed their babes against trees and fell upon their spears. But as they were only ignorant savages, of course there was nothing heroic about this. It was mere stupid obstinacy and contumacy, a bestial rejection of the messages of the Prince of Peace.

Both the Kings of Spain and the Popes, as temporal and spiritual sovereigns of mankind, enacted wise and temperate measures for the treatment of their "dear children and subjects," the "savages." They appointed respectable governors and placed the new-found savages under the protection of an order of monks. Unluckily, apparently neither the spiritual nor the temporal sovereign's authority extended across the Atlantic. The governors and the monks were either impotent or connived at the atrocities. Then, when the damage was done, and the virtual extinction of both Caribs and Arawaks certain, the good bishop Las Casas made his "startling revelations." Modern Spanish historians say they are exaggerated. Perhaps they are—but where are the Caribs and the Arawaks, once numbered by hundreds of thousands? An insignificant remnant.

ARTIFEX: SKETCHES AND IDEAS

It was Las Casas who, in the tenderness of his heart and finding that the Indians wouldn't work, suggested the forcible importation of negroes from Africa. The Lord knows why, unless he relied on the text about Ham serving in the tents of Shem, about which of course the unfortunate Hams were quite ignorant. But the idea was taken up with enthusiasm, and soon the African slave trade was in full blast—with the English not among the least modest in profiting by it. I won't go into details, they are too sickening and frightful; but if you want to be ashamed of the human race, just read some of the contemporary accounts of this monstrous "trade." The balance of trade—I wonder how it works out between whitest Europe and darkest Africa?

Whatever may be true or false in the previous paragraphs (I can speak only from what I have read) there can be no doubt whatever that Abel's progenitors did not make the long journey from Africa first class in a liner—they came against their will in the fetid hold of a slaver. One can visualize it all—the sleeping African village, the sudden terror caused by the irruption of the English cut-throats, men, women and children carried off indiscriminately, the chain gang to the coast, the long awful journey chained in the hold, the sea-sickness, the stench, the semi-starvation, the hideous overcrowding, the daily deaths with the "plop" overboard and the sharks. Happy were they who died. Unluckily for them and for us, they didn't all die; and they possessed neither that pestilential fighting obstinacy of the Caribs nor the suicidal stupidity of the Arawaks. They were meek—and some of them lived. . . .

But all this has been settled, liquidated long ago. Emancipation—has it been settled? It seems to me that Emancipation only dealt with a part of the problem, that of forced labour. It hasn't settled the problem of the real (not legal fiction) status and the future of these hundreds of thousands of coloured people who have come to think of these parts as their home

ABEL

and who would be miserable and bewildered if forcibly deported to their continent of origin. What is going to happen?

If I try to answer that question, I see I shall involve myself in a mess of politics, sociology, anthropology, economics and what-not, in dealing with which I should only show my ignorance and my incompetence. It is better for me to stick to Abel and what I can see. So far as Abel is concerned personally I think he's all right, provided he continues to have good Masters in the future as he obviously must have had in the past. But Abel is admittedly one of a very small minority, and I have the feeling that future Abels will find out the sham of the white superiority, find it isn't something intrinsic and godlike (as he thinks) but merely a set of clever tricks which can be easily learned and diabolically used by other races—the Japanese, for instance. And since the negroes really haven't a money sense, they can't be expected to worship our God.

What about the others—all the lying and tricking and thieving and slacking ones who haven't got Abel's touching faith in the white Master as a son of the gods, who are really always in a state of grudging resentment against necessary authority—like the Mexicans—and are only kept quiescent by that grey silent destroyer which comes creeping unexpectedly along the coast? What about them? In some places they outnumber the whites in the startling proportion of 250 to one. They don't serve the white Masters willingly, they are always jeering and trying to cheat them, trying to wear the white Masters down by hindering as far as they dare. And in this they are wrong, because the white Masters still do think and plan for them. Without the Masters I think they would fall into a brutal chaos in which the good ones, like Abel, would be the first to suffer. On the other hand, they might not. But how long will the destroyer's successors continue to creep from under the headland, how long will that island in the North Sea continue to send out generation after generation of men to carry out the

ARTIFEX: SKETCHES AND IDEAS

weary and rather thankless task of keeping these particular cogs in the machine running? For now they are only cogs in the great money machine, and that seems doomed beyond question of appeal. Perhaps some more successful competitor will begin the hopeless weary task of sending men and destroyers—how well named, but they ought to be called self-destroyers. Perhaps nobody will send, and then the coloured people who already potentially own these districts through sheer weight of numbers will actually own them. Perhaps after all the meek will inherit the earth.

Purpose in Life

Purpose in Life

STRICTLY speaking we can't say that life is "for" anything. Life is. There is no answer to the question Why is it? There is not even anything but a conjectural answer to the question How did it occur? According to one theory, which still has adherents, God, having spent infinite ages in idleness and solitude, suddenly created heaven and earth in the year 4004 B.C., for the benefit of the Jews. By an extension of franchise in or about the year A.D. 1, the Christians were admitted, with the remarkable concession that if they behaved themselves in certain ways they would live for ever after they were dead in the joys of contemplation and music. You have only to observe the average Christian to discover how fitted he is for these two pursuits and how much he would enjoy an eternity of them. Many modifications of this theory have been introduced to save the appearances—the picturesque date of 4004 B.C. is abandoned—but nothing has yet been said to make the Christian Heaven attractive. What is inconceivable is that any one should regret it. According to this theory the "purpose" of life is to save one's soul, *i.e.*, to invest life here in the hopes of eternal interest. A sordid calculation.

But we have another theory, which also has a picturesque date—two thousand million years. This at one and the same

ARTIFEX: SKETCHES AND IDEAS

time gratifies the contemporary love of a peak quotation and leaves plenty of "time" for things to happen. But what are two thousand million years, and what is "time" anyway? And how do you measure "a year" when the earth is still part of the sun and therefore cannot revolve round it in $365\frac{1}{4}$ days? And then? Ah then—the picturesque waves of fiery gas cooling to liquid with picturesque bits of slag boiling about on top; the picturesque primeval ocean lapping a muddy shore under a fierier sun richer in ultra-violet rays, carbon, oxygen, hydrogen, hey presto! protoplasm. Miraculous stuff, protoplasm. I take off my hat to Herr Protoplasm, I'm sure he was a nordic blond. Hail! revered parent of me and the megatherium, ancestor of the pterodactyl and the bug, androgynous split-arse, mother of universities and father of the poor! Not Rule Britannia, but Evolve Protoplasm. Two thousand million years of strugforlife, natural and sexual (?) selection (??) to produce nineteenth-century England. Darwin, thou should'st be a-living at this hour. And the moral of *that* is: Be a good philoprogenitive citizen, be a poop in fact.

Meanwhile, there's our life here, absurd, mysterious, agonizing, delicious, futile life. Who has not cursed the hour of his conception and the day of his birth? And who has not at some time or other in a warm gust of exuberance blessed the old fool that begot him? In a hundred years' time nobody will know or care that we ever existed, but meanwhile we're here, and see the show for nothing. I admit it is rather like paying a hundred dollars to sit for ten minutes on a rickety stool in a verminous theatre which is giving a ten-day Chinese drama. We don't know what went before or what is to come and don't understand the language, but there's no need to shoot the actors, they're doing their best. Personally I don't set much store on being the heir of all the ages; it seems to me they've chiefly debts to bequeath. But if there is any fun in the show, I'm for it. If you find amusement in protoplasm or in the thought that I

PURPOSE IN LIFE

shall go to hell and you'll go to heaven, amuse-toi donc, "cré nom!

"Life is real, life is earnest..."

My dear Citizen, do you really believe that? Real! Real this animula, blandula, vagula, real this tremulous rainbow of consciousness, this pinch of lighted dust that flashes? Life is the most unreal thing imaginable. There are simply no precedents whatever for it in the Universal Laws discovered for us by our scientific betters. It's an accident, a freak, a lark, a holiday between two eternities of nothing. What is real is that enormous uninhabited universe which, believe me, will outlast us both. We're a kind of joke. If you don't believe it, read the scientists. So why be earnest? Don't feel responsible for the universe—it wasn't your doing. Don't feel responsible for the Empire—it can disappear without your assistance. Take it easy. Go to the plumber's mate, consider his ways, and be wise.

Nevertheless, although life is not "for" anything and no indisputable "purpose" increasing or otherwise can be discovered, considerable credit is due to human ingenuity in the invention of "purposes." Civilization is the art of agreeing to believe in invented purposes. A civilization which admitted the purposeless nature of life would probably collapse—there must be some sort of carrot in front of the donkey's nose. I am tempted to formulate a law of civilization in these terms: The vigour and duration of a community vary in inverse ratio to the reasonableness and feasibility of its purpose.

There is a school of thought which holds that the first civilization was that of Egypt, and that it was organized for the fantastic purpose of making the Pharaoh immortal. It is believed that Osiris was the engineer-agriculturist who founded the system of Nile irrigation. When this remarkable man died he was deified and made immortal, not for his own good and reward,

ARTIFEX: SKETCHES AND IDEAS

but merely that he might continue his services from the other world. It worked, it worked marvellously. (One wonders what absurdity wouldn't work with the curious imbeciles that we are.) Every Pharaoh in turn had to be deified. Then, owing to the law of democracy or too much of a good thing, every guttersnipe had to be immortal. Much too precious to be lost. This worked well, until it over-reached itself by being too logical. When the High Priest of the immortality-makers became Pharaoh, it was the end of Egyptian civilization as a creative force—henceforth that came from outside.

What shall I do to inherit eternal life? is still the perpetual naïf question, involving a huge *petitio principii*. To paraphrase Renan, the sucker is indeed immortal. The Mohammedans desolated large tracts of the earth for centuries in a fruitless but spirited effort to cause every one to be circumcized, and thus go to heaven. They lasted about a thousand years; the Egyptians, a far less aggressive people, about four thousand. On the other hand, take the Athenians. Their local deity Athena—who subsequently turned up much disguised as Hagia Sophia—represented the cult of wisdom. The republic didn't last three centuries, and poor Robespierre's goddess of Reason was a flop from the beginning. Yet the irrational Yaveh, who is a detestable barbarian, still has adherents. Which leads to the reflection that fanaticism is the greatest human force yet discovered, though hitherto it has always eventually defeated itself. Nobody can be fanatical about what is self-evident and rational—hence the "purpose" of a civilization must always be vague, unprovable and unattainable. When one "purpose" ceases to deceive another is invented. But in my opinion the first one was the best, it is so staggeringly impudent. The genius who thought of "eternal life" as a carrot for the multitude has my unfeigned respect.

The Roman Empire appears to have been founded on the Teutonic delusion that military power makes a community

PURPOSE IN LIFE

superior to all decency and all rivals. The Romans proved their superiority by adopting the civilization of the "conquered" Hellenes. Constantine, a man of genius if a blackguard, tried to preserve the Empire by grafting on to it an interesting syncretism of Life and Death cults, included a revived version of "eternal life." The Empire vanished, but the fanaticism remained. Europe escaped a theocracy through its vices, which only goes to show the danger of being too virtuous.

If I may be allowed a mixed metaphor I should say that in comparison with the old original carrot of "eternal life" more recent "life purposes" have been rather small potatoes. Liberty, for instance. The French went on the rampage about it in the 1790's and liberated whole peoples by looting them. Liberté, Egalité, Fraternité sound good and are pleasantly vague. Ask a modern Frenchman what he thinks about them—that is, if you like listening to invective. And when you go to France don't forget to fill your fountain pen ready for those forms. Liberty—it kept Europe in a turmoil through most of the nineteenth century, and as a catch-word now it wouldn't bring a dozen geese across the road.

Then there is the "greatest happiness of the greatest number"—there is something about the "pursuit of Happiness" in the Constitution of the United States. This was a happy formula, but unluckily the emphasis has been on the number instead of the happiness. Happiness was far too rational a purpose, so it was decided that numerosity is bliss. Hence the vogue for quantity and hyperbolical statistics. There are patriots who would feel a thrill of pride if they were told—no need to prove it—that the fleas of their nation are larger and better-nourished than those of any other nation, and if placed nose to tail would go three times round the equator. Happy fleas. Happy nation.

Nationalism is another of these carrots, with a peculiar and dangerous quality—it is liable to explode and blow the don-

ARTIFEX: SKETCHES AND IDEAS

keys' heads off, and also unluckily the heads of any few sensible people who may happen to be alive at the time. The strength of nationalism is in its extreme silliness. There are about seventy "sovereign states" in the world each of which is superior to all the others—within its own boundaries—and must be armed to the full extent of its exchequer (and a bit beyond) for defence. Seventy-odd Ajaxes, all strictly on the defensive! A comic spectacle, if the fools weren't so serious about it and in possession of such lethal weapons. Like ill-bred urchins they yell at each other: Yah! we're better than you are. And sooner or later, like urchins, they are bound to get into a scuffle about it. Whereupon the defeated urchins rearm defensively for revenge, and the triumphant urchins continue armed defensively to preserve the hard-won peace. Both scream louder than ever: Yah! etcetera. Taking a leaf from the Mohammedan book, nationalists are now seriously arguing that every valiant nationalist who dies fighting for my-country-right-or-wrong goes straight to Valhalla. It is my earnest prayer that every valiant nationalist may go to Valhalla—soon.

Undoubtedly I should be accused of bourgeois bias if I omitted to notice that succulent and sanguinary carrot of our time, the dictatorship of the proletariat. It must ever be a heart-warming thought to imagine the hundred million or more enviable proletarians who have conquered this right by no uncommon exertions and effusion of blood, rising up each morning and thinking to themselves as they shave—or do not shave —What shall we dictate today? How shall we dictate it? To whom shall we dictate? What a touching example of human goodness and unanimity may here be held up to mankind, seeing that these dictators invariably dictate that they shall do what the government tells them at the government rate of pay! "It is excellent to have a giant's strength," they say, "but . . . look out, the cop's coming." No, I may have peculiar tastes, but I would rather pay my four and six in the pound to His Majesty

PURPOSE IN LIFE

than exercise my prerogative of dictatorship on such terms.

"No unbiassed observer, who derives pleasure from the welfare of his species, can fail to consider the long and uninterruptedly increasing prosperity of England as the most beautiful phenomenon in the history of mankind."

Possibly you may think I invented that as a bit of nastiness. Well, I didn't, though I wish I had thought of that "beautiful phenomenon." As a matter of fact, it's a quotation from Hallam's *Middle Ages*. People make a great mistake in not reading the Victorians (the book in question was published in the reign of George III, but never mind) who are the greatest humourists on record. Your "purpose" in life as a shareholder in this beautiful phenomenon is easily analyzed into individual and collective, in peace and in war. In peace your individual purpose is to make money (or merely earn your living if you've no more gumption than that) and behave as a brainless, insensitive but inoffensive jackass; and your collective purpose is to pay taxes and shut up about it. In war your individual purpose is to find a cushy job; and (if you can't) your collective purpose is to get yourself unhandsomely cut up by generals of genius and-thank-god-we've-got-a-navy.

There remains the "purpose" of exerting power which naturally is only possible to a very tiny minority of human beings, at least in the form of sovereign power. Everybody seems to want to command something, if it's only a husband or wife or an animal. Wretched is he who can command nothing, influence nothing, is forced to admit himself a complete zero in power. This is the impulse which is artfully exploited for all the delusive collective "purposes." The formula of the power-seeker is always the same, however concealed in verbiage: Submit to me and I will make you master. Follow me and I will give you eternal life; follow me and I will give you power over your enemies; follow me and I will give you the power of

ARTIFEX: SKETCHES AND IDEAS

riches. And then what? Nobody stops to ask, so why give the obvious answer?

The exercise of sovereign power seems to be the one sufficing "purpose." It grows by what it feeds on. An incompetent may abdicate without much reluctance, but even he is likely to ride rusty like Mr. Roper's elephants. Diocletian is a great exception. Certainly there are chagrins attached to power, for there seems to be a mysterious law by which every act of power weaves an invisible fetter. You can see Bonaparte and Caesar weaving the net of power to catch themselves. The lesson is not yet learned. Observe the acts of modern governments, arbitrary or elected—how many of them are actually intended to conserve or to extend their power or their tenure of power, how few devoted to any intelligent concern for the happiness of the governed? Nor is that surprising when the majority idea of happiness is a rise of income. Any government is delighted for you to become rich—taxes and death-duties—but they don't care a bean about your happiness. And the one government which won't let you become rich has a weird idea of happiness.

How far do power-wielders believe in the "purposes" they dangle before their subjects? A question to be asked. On the face of it one would suppose them to be far too shrewd to be duped by these illusions, and that the strength of governments lies in their cynicism. But it depends on circumstances. The earlier Pharaohs evidently believed in their own godship and immortality—that was their strength. Later, when the delusion became evident to the few and was merely a device of government, their strength lay in not believing it but pretending to officially. Aknaton paid the penalty of being sincere in his beliefs. It was necessary for Queen Elizabeth to pose as the champion of religion; it would have been disastrous for her to believe in any one of the silly sects—the mistake made by Charles I. But—to jump to our time—it was necessary for Mussolini to believe in his Fascism (the doctrine of which he

PURPOSE IN LIFE

has invented with skilful opportunism) because Italy needed a "purpose." And yet, does he believe in it? So able a man must, one feels, occasionally see through his own bunk. And in all old countries cynicism is the handmaid of power.

There is something morbid about extreme arbitrary power—it always gets involved in death, and leads its followers to death. When you are a man-god, responsible only to a far-off deity, the knowledge that the fell sergeant inevitable awaits you is maddening. What is the good of being a god among men if you must resign your godship to an impatient heir? Embrace death or flee from death—it is all one. Philip II went to bed every night over his own sepulchre; Louis XIV would not go to St. Germain because the towers of St. Denis are there visible. Yet there is a hideous odour of death about both Versailles and the Escorial, not solely due to the fact that the latter is a burial place and both stand in melancholy abandonment. The palace of Urbino, even more abandoned to desolation, is a cheerful inspiring place, with a sweet savour of life. But the Power above all power is Death, and the power-lovers know it. Their memory stinks like a corpse.

Under these general "purposes" there exists the multitude of minor individual "purposes" ranging from golf to a grand passion. To discover and to explain them is one of the functions of novelists; and since sexual desire in its infinity of forms is undoubtedly the most frequent of these "purposes," the most intensely experienced, the most fertile in "situations," there need be no surprise that it forms the main theme of most novels. Money and women are the private interests of mankind—the rest is sports and hobbies. Unluckily Antony and Cleopatra do not flourish in a civilization of suburbs, and on analysis so many "purposes" turn out to be merely a form of money-worship. There is no genuine phallus-worship, so that even that potent and mysterious god is domesticated or trivial. Life is run on the

ARTIFEX: SKETCHES AND IDEAS

hire-purchase system, under the auspices of insurance and advertising.

Money-making as a "purpose" has its points. The money-maker is always going to retire and "live my own life," but he can always postpone this desperate resolution on the plea that he hasn't yet got enough money. Safety first. How many men I have known who went into business or the professions, assuring me that as soon as they had "a nice little lump of capital" they intended to retire and live happy ever after. Some have disappeared—down and out probably—others have got their nice little lumps, pretty big in some cases, but they still go on. The fact is, they are now afraid to give up. They wouldn't know what to do with life if they had it. The only thing for them to do is to go on "making" money. Like the snake with his tail in his mouth. As for the successful but superannuated business man who is enjoying the mellow evening of life—well, that note of wretched pathos has been struck before now. . . .

There is no "purpose" in life. It is an end in itself. To realize this is already a major success, but there is no formula for the enjoyment of consciousness.

Freedom of the Press

Freedom of the Press

THIS is a fly-blown and moth-eaten subject, and yet there may be something left to say.

Theoretically the printing press—not merely the daily press—is "free" in

> "*A land where girt by friends or foes*
> *A man may speak the thing he will.*"

But just try it in print, my dear Tennyson, and see what happens. Just try it. The English law of libel was apparently designed for the discouragement of fiction, and the plaintiff always wins unless he happens to be an author. Most publishers and many novelists are at some time or other blackmailed by means of the law of libel. Newspapers are mulcted of enormous sums for telling the truth about insignificant persons, even when it is proved to the hilt that the lapse into truth was entirely unintentional.

Some novelists try feebly to protect themselves by announcing on the fly-leaf that all their characters are "entirely imaginary." This always suggests to me—and it sometimes turns out to be true—that the imaginary characters in question are malevolent caricatures of the author's closest friends. I should really like to see an entirely imaginary character. What would it be? Are there any in literature? Caliban and Ariel, perhaps, and amateur detectives, but they would not make satisfactory novels. All characters are the result of conscious and unconscious observation. It is axiomatic. What say the Scholastics? Nihil in intellectu quod non prius in sensu. Q.E.D. Martians, men in the moon, inhabitants of Utopias are notoriously unsatisfactory as "characters." Willy-nilly we draw the life about us, and a historical novel may be indebted for its local colour to a Bloomsbury binge. The law of libel is a sword of Damocles to us all. Touching wood, it has not yet fallen on me; but then I have the unimpeachable evidence of some of my most distinguished rivals to prove that I "can't draw character."

Unluckily literature is not a matter for experts or for expert testimony, at least according to the practice of the English courts of Law, the envy and admiration of the whole world, etcetera, etcetera. The opinion of informers and policemen (who have graduated in the school of life) is preferred. If they don't know dirt when they see it, who will? I was once present in a foreign court when a charge of publishing an alleged obscene book was tried, at the instigation of the British, by the way. The magistrate was a Daniel. "What is all this about?" cried he, turning over a portentous dossier. "I must have expert witnesses. Am I to decide these fine points of literary tact?" Whereupon he charged two literary friends of the defendant to examine and report upon the said obscene libel. Result: case dismissed. A Daniel, I say.

Obscenity is of course the great joke, but one likely to prove expensive and disagreeable to an unlucky author. I believe there does exist a legal definition of "obscenity." I can't remember the exact words, but it is something like this—"obscenity is that which is likely to provoke lust in those likely to be lustful." A definition worthy of Bouvard and Pécuchet. I tremble for

FREEDOM OF THE PRESS

Cleopatra's needle, a monstrous thing, all said and done, to set before ladies. Read not the tale of Lot and his daughters. . . . Behold, thou art fair, my beloved, thou hast dove's eyes—take them away, they make the company lustful.

Is it the inflammability of the subject or the combustion of the object which is legally reprehensible? If the former, let the subject look to herself—I presume she is the *jeune fille*. Some one remarked to Dr. Samuel Johnson that Lord Tomnoddy said Prior's poems were obscene. "Then sir," said the Doctor, "Lord Tomnoddy must be more *combustible* than other men." Doubtless he sat upon the bench and grew warm in consequence.

It is to be observed that recently in England prosecutions for obscenity have been brought against artists but never against scientists. The scandal of the prosecution of Havelock Ellis's *Psychology of Sex* presumably taught a lesson to Messieurs the smut-hunters. It is typical of our time that it should have no respect for an artist until he has become a dotard and a Grand Old Woman. Nobody cares when an artist is dragged down in the ignominy of a law court before an illiterate magistrate; few indeed even realize that the odium of scandal for the prosecutions of Joyce and Lawrence is with the prosecutors. Hatred of art is innate with the common man, and for him the artist is an outlaw. It is an honourable estate in such circumstances.'

The scientist is honoured. Why? Because for the middleheads "science" is equivalent to profitable invention. There's money in it, and where there is money there is sanctity. Call your subject biology, physiology, psychology, psychopathology, sexology even—so long as it has an "ology" in it—and write yourself D.Sc., L.R.C.P., M.D., and you may print with impunity facts and speculations, a hundredth part of which would bring an artist to ignominy and punishment. Is it a condition of art in England that the artist must be ignorant and

ARTIFEX: SKETCHES AND IDEAS

flatter the prejudices of the ignorant? Human beings are the subject of the artist as well as of the psychologist and the biologist. Must the artist know nothing of what the scientists can teach him? Oh, so long as the artist is *decent*. . . . My dear sir, do you imagine that biology is "decent?" I quote from a book in common circulation, *not* one of those labelled for the medical profession only:

> "Homosexuality has been regarded as the state in which an individual equipped with all the physical characters appropriate to one sex exhibits the psychological characters appropriate to the opposite sex. Thus a homosexual male was looked upon as being psychologically female, though structurally male. It was natural that against the background of our knowledge of the relation of the endocrine glands and the sex characters, it should be assumed that homosexuality was to be attributed to the secretion on the part of the gonad of the wrong sex-hormone; that is to say, that a testis, instead of elaborating male sex-hormone, was producing female sex-hormone, and vice-versa . . . it is commonly forgotten that there is no real reason why the homosexual should be essentially different from the heterosexual. It is well known that the male of domesticated animals, under certain conditions, very frequently attempts to perform the act of sexual congress with other males. If twelve cocks are kept together, in the absence of females, it is certain that some of these males will be treated by the rest as though they were females. Homosexuality does not consist so much in differences in male behaviour as in the choice of unusual objects. . . . It would seem therefore that homosexuality is not so much due to a disturbance in the secretions of the endocrine glands, but rather to a disturbance of the central nervous system which results in the choice of an unusual object for the purposes of mating."

I have shortened the passage of illustrative matter, and cannot forbear pointing out that the learned author appears to ignore the existence of female homosexuality (the "homo" is the Greek "homos" not the Latin "homo"). I chose the passage deliberately because it shows how a Professor of Genetics is allowed to write openly and for popular reading on a subject which is practically forbidden to an artist. The mere mention of female homosexuality in England is sufficient to ensure the refusal of a licence to a play or the prosecution of a novel. A sneer or snigger may be allowed, but not a serious effort to understand and portray.

Homosexuality is not a subject I wish to treat myself, although it would provide a novelist with situations dramatic, pathetic and tragical. On the other hand it is plain that people need instruction in this matter. I have seen the statement somewhere that as many as one per cent. of the total population are homosexuals. In any event it is barbarous and ignorant to punish people for "a disturbance in the secretions of the endocrine glands," or "a disturbance of the central nervous system." And if a novelist tries to present such characters with understanding it is still more barbarous and ignorant to rave about "obscenity" and prussic acid.

The material of science and art is the same—the whole known universe. Both seek to tell the truth, but artistic truth is very different from scientific truth. Sometimes they are complementary, sometimes they may contradict each other. Both are valuable, and neither is really esteemed in the modern world. We tacitly admit that truth is the aim of art by using "false" as the final adjective of disparagement to an artist. I have read an interesting defence of the novel, based on a theory that the novel form forces a writer to tell the truth—he may think he is saying something quite different, but the form will make him unconsciously reveal the truth. It is a large assumption, for it assumes sincerity. But if he is not "sincere" he is not an artist. Confusion has been introduced by using such words as "feigning" to express the imaginative process. The "feigning" is only for the purpose of illustrating subtler truths beyond externals, as a symbol may be "feigned" but hides or reveals a truth. The Ode to a Nightingale is not ornithological truth. Indeed, if Keats had put into his poem what some ornithologists say about the nightingale's song (*i.e.*, that it is an expression of sex)

ARTIFEX: SKETCHES AND IDEAS

he would probably have been called "obscene" for attributing such impulses to an innocent songster.

In any case it is a poor sort of civilization which allows the arts to be maimed and artists to be persecuted in the name of obsolete prejudices. The Popes did not persecute Michelangelo for painting Leda and the Swan, but some of our journalists tried to make a stink about the picture being hung in the National Gallery. The idea didn't catch on—they hadn't the sense to see that officials and not artists were involved. Had there been a living artist to hamper and annoy, it would have been taken up with enthusiasm. In England it is much more honourable to be the keeper of other people's pictures than to be able to paint. Homage is not paid to the artist, but to the artist's success. The street through which Cimabue's picture was carried with rejoicings was named the Borgo Allegro. We have no such street in London, unless it be the road to Tyburn.

The three art forms most interfered with in practice are the cinema, the theatre and the novel. The first two are openly censored, and there is a good deal of indirect censorship of novels, far more than is generally supposed. Prosecution is rarely used, except as a last resource, because of the publicity given. Prosecution tends to defeat its own end, because the book is immediately pirated abroad and many copies are smuggled into England by heroic undergraduates. Of course, publisher, printer and author suffer financial loss, which is gratifying. But the book circulates. Sneaky methods are therefore preferred, consonant with the character of informers, such as indirect boycott. But as even these often prove ineffective, there is agitation for a censor of novels.

Why novels only? Why not poetry and essays? Why the cinema and theatre? It is obvious. These are the popular, lively forms, through which a large body of people may be influenced. Also, they are effective substitutes for religion. Art is a religion older than religion. The cave paintings of Altamira are older

FREEDOM OF THE PRESS

than any known religion, which was possibly invented and certainly organized in pre-Dynastic Egypt. Religious significance has been read into the bison and boar and deer of Altamira. It may be so, but one might equally well maintain that the paintings were art for art's sake. Hebraism has always been at war with the arts, and they survived Christianity only because it was imposed on artistic peoples. And because art is co-existent with human life. Even the Catholic Church was chiefly interested in art as propaganda, like the present Russian government. Malatesta was excommunicated for that beautiful church of his at Rimini. Wherever there is Christianity the arts must subserve or be persecuted, and where there is Catholicism the sciences also.

There seems to be no coherent body of principles governing censorship, whether open or sneaky. In Ireland and Australia it seems to be a matter of religious prejudice; in Germany and Italy a form of political bullying. But inevitably prohibition brings bootlegging—there is a considerable underground traffic in forbidden wares. Even in pure England there is a stealthy market for deplorably vulgar and inartistic films of a sexual kind. I say "deplorable," because treatment of sex motives should be noble and serious, as in the ancient world and the Renaissance. But one must not be pedantic—there is room for Aristophanes and Voltaire.

I think we can say that the unacknowledged principle of censorship is a matter for the psychologists to investigate. It is a form of Sadism, finding satisfaction in the repression and destruction of what it thinks would give pleasure to others—like the pure-souled gentlemen who wanted to "purify" the goldfinch by pulling out its bright feathers. Besides, an ugly world is good for trade. So far as England is concerned the line of procedure seems to be this: If a book is likely to be widely read—and any novel may be—and if in its general tendency it is a criticism of officially accepted values, and especially if it tends

ARTIFEX: SKETCHES AND IDEAS

to substitute other values, then it is closely scanned for passages which can be labelled "indecent." The law being so extremely vague and magistrates what they are, almost any passage of a sexual kind may be construed as indecent. In other words the indecency charge is often a pretext.

Oddly enough, "indecency" may be a matter of style, another proof of the innate English dislike for art. A conventional-minded author will have a conventional style. But style, says Remy de Gourmont, is thinking, feeling, seeing intensely, vividly, originally. Thus, the description of a sexual episode by a conventional-minded author will be in vague worn clichés which have no effect on the imagination. Exactly the same situation described by a stylist will be vivid and seem new. Instead of a faint flicker—Hullo, now they're off to bed—the reader sees and feels the emotions and sensations of the protagonists vividly. The one is bad art, and therefore decent, the other good art, and therefore indecent.

Let me give examples of how this works out. Here is an extract from a decent novel:

"As some children of a miracle, they stood heart to heart to tell their story anew, to seal in one sustained caress the bond of love he had written for them.
" 'Fekla, beloved, mine, mine! I will not say goodnight to you.'
" 'Ivor—husband—the night is no more.'
"The new day, indeed, had dawned—the enduring day of their desire."

And so, as Mr. Pepys remarked, to bed. The chastity of the *jeune fille* reader is saved. But how? Apart from having her sensibility perverted by the excruciatingly trashy and false writing—a serious matter—she is left (may we assume) wondering how Fekla and Ivor "sealed in one sustained caress the bond of love." The "day of their desire" you observe is "enduring"—likely to mislead the *jeune fille* in an important concern. But as the whole scene is sentimental bunk, it is "decent."

FREEDOM OF THE PRESS

Here is a passage from another novel which was actually condemned as "obscene" for the pages from which this extract is taken:

"She had her moments of exaltation still, re-births of old exaltations. As she sat by her bedroom window, watching the steady rain, her spirit was somewhere far off.

"She sat in pride and curious pleasure. When there was no one to exult with, and the unsatisfied soul must dance and play, then one danced before the Unknown.

"Suddenly she realized that this was what she wanted to do. Big with child as she was, she danced there in the bedroom by herself, lifting her hands and her body to the Unseen, to the unseen Creator who had chosen her to Whom she belonged.

"She would not have had any one know. She danced in secret, and her soul rose in bliss. She danced in secret before the Creator, she took off her clothes and danced in pride of her bigness."

Here is a situation the reverse of banal. Notice the precision of the writing—no mixed metaphors here, no children of a miracle sealing a bond of love in a sustained caress. You cannot say there is any dwelling on the carnal, yet the mere power of the writing forces you to see the naked woman dancing. There is pathos in the scene. A pregnant wife is estranged from her husband, yet cannot submit to be quenched in her pride as the bearer of new life. Someone must be glad and praise her that she is with child. So, in her solitude, she dances before the Unknown God of breeding women, naked as David danced uncovered before the ark of the Lord. If her husband will not rejoice with her, then the God of all new life will accept her and rejoice with her. It is the religion of mothers—that God will praise them for their children.

Now, in the name of common sense, can such a thing be called libidinous, lascivious, indecent, obscene? Is it "obscene" for a lonely woman to be glad she is with child, and to offer herself naked before the God of life? Is it because she is naked?

ARTIFEX: SKETCHES AND IDEAS

But presumably she is as naked to God in her clothes as out of them. She didn't dance naked before men. She offered herself, her sacred nakedness, to God. And, as usual, God did nothing about it, so we don't know His opinion. But why argue? The evidence is plain.

But let us suppose that the passage had run thus:

"Maddened by her husband's coldness and neglect she suspected he was unfaithful. She took from its hiding place the revolver given her by her soldier brother to protect her honour, and with unshaken hand fired four shots at the betrayer's back. He staggered, his hands wildly clawing the air, then collapsed and lay still—dead!"

That's O.K., fine, stuff to give 'em. Nothing obscene there— merely a spot of murder. And murder is clean. It is obscene to rejoice in the quickening of life, clean to inflict death. What an Augean stable is the common mind!

It might be worth the while of a competent psychologist to investigate carefully the hidden mind processes which have contributed to the vogue of the crime and detective story. Murder, it is true, has been the subject of great art, but only when treated with a deep sense of responsibility and almost religious awe. Moreover, the attention of the spectator is turned away from the mere brutal act of slaughter and the scarcely less brutal pursuit of the murderer, to dwell upon the state of mind which makes so terrible an act possible, and upon the moral problem of blood-guiltiness. In the trilogy of Aeschylus we suffer the unbearable agony of Orestes and find an answer to the question: When must revenge for blood-guiltiness cease? Again, in Macbeth we contemplate the mind of the murderer from ambition, led on fatally from crime to crime until the whole structure of his blood-built greatness crashes. And in the contemplation of great tragedy, where the murderer is always a potentially noble spirit, there is really a catharsis. We live through deep passions and agonies, and are purged to humility and peace.

FREEDOM OF THE PRESS

The murder stories of our stage and fiction are entirely different. There is little characterization, no sense of moral responsibility, no great principle illustrated, no exploration of the Hinterland der Seele. The whole thing hinges on a corpse and is a corpse. Indeed it might be argued that as the ridiculous puppets of these works never come alive, they cannot be killed. But that would be overlooking the fact that the *sensation* of murder is enjoyed for its own sake. The murderer now becomes the victim of a vicarious lynch, and the reader enjoys further sensations of a very disgusting kind in watching him tracked down. It is a cold-blooded jig-saw puzzle, if you like, but unless there is the spice of brutality, unless blood is supposed to be shed, there would be no book. Really, it is very nasty. And very stupid.

I find myself in disagreement with those who believe that art is a species of play or a semi-obsolete survival of religious ritual. Art is a flowering of the life impulse. It is as useless as a flower and as life itself—and as useful. But as the life impulse itself may turn to death and self-destruction, so may art. There is an art of the death impulse. Normally art is associated with the sexual impulse, not only by an analogy of creativeness but because the sexual impulse is itself so closely associated with vitality; and also with religion, which is the quest for life. An art form so stereotyped, so poverty-stricken in all but jig-saw puzzle inventiveness as the murder story, must respond to some psychological need. I suggest it arises from the suppression of the vital impulse along with the sexual impulse and the natural (not revealed) religious impulse. Our society is based on the repression of those impulses for the benefit of commerce, war and social organization. Consequently the reader of the murder story is really witnessing the murder of his own self, and takes his revenge in joining vicariously the pursuers of his murderer. The symbolism is obvious if you analyze almost any contemporary murder story, and the insatiable appetite for endless

ARTIFEX: SKETCHES AND IDEAS

repetitions of the same symbolical situation shows how deep the repression must go.

So many books are published, so few have any of the flame of the vital creative impulse. The few that are produced are almost drowned in the flood of catchpenny imitations and negative books. There is as much criticism of poetry, for instance, as poetry and attempts at poetry, if not more. And this criticism is seldom an attempt to communicate enthusiasm as in Longinus; more often an exercise in the analytic method of Aristotle; but generally merely negative. They find a formula of denigration and rest upon it. The purpose of criticism as now practised would seem to be finding reasons for *not* admiring—which, as Byron remarked, seems no great happiness. It is much the same with all the arts. The one unanswerable form of criticism, to do better, is not popular. Yet that surely was the method in the creative epochs of Athens and Florence. The artist today is a lonely and discouraged person struggling against the tide.

This is a period of great scientific triumph. Quand on a de la force on en met partout is possibly a false statement, and it may be impossible for a society to excel both in the sciences and the arts. The history of civilization would seem to show an alternation of epochs of technical discovery and epochs of artistic creativeness. The former must be thoroughly absorbed before the latter is set free. Is it untrue to say that our scientifically great epoch is artistically mean and poor? It is prolific but not powerful. Even among the not inconsiderable number whom one respects as artists of integrity there is rather a high level of good mediocrity than great indisputable achievement. Between the monied amateur and the money-seeking professional the arts wither. Yet science can never take the place of art. Their aims are so different, and the source of the art impulse so deep it can only be finally stopped with life itself. But

FREEDOM OF THE PRESS

where life is poor—and how poor in life we are!—art must be impoverished too.

I should have liked to live in an epoch of great artists, even if it were not granted me to be the humblest among them. I should like to live in an age that was passionately creative, where society was as deeply stirred by high achievements of the creative spirit as it is now by trade, war and invention. Yes, there is a stark horrible beauty in a great battleship, a rigid grace in an airplane, a Rue de la Paix elegance in a stream-lined motor-car and a platinum bracelet, and the skyscrapers are undoubtedly higher than the streets of Venice. And yes, I have read the peppy ads. in the *Saturday Evening Post*, I have contemplated the pylons of the electric grid, I have danced to jazz, and I have seen the greatest artillery barrage yet produced. I have seen Middlesborough and Cannes, I have been in an ocean liner and crossed vast steel suspension bridges; I know the comfort of a good dinner in Paris. And my soul cries out against it all and is unsatisfied. I am not satisfied to say that after all, somme tout, all said and done, machinery is art, and call it quits. Music is music, not noise; painting is painting, not poster-work or abstraction; sculpture is sculpture, not rock-drilling; architecture is architecture, not engineering, literature is literature, not writing ads.; poetry is poetry, not word-mosaics. . . . I want music, painting, sculpture, architecture, literature, poetry.

And compared with the grief of that lack, the existence of a censorship of books seems a very trivial matter.

A Renaissance Aryan
(Condensed from the Italian of Bandello)

A Renaissance Aryan

(Condensed from the Italian of Bandello)

IN THE reign of King Ferdinand a Spanish minor friar, named Fra Francisco, arrived in Naples to preach. This friar was a brutal ignorant fellow, but he was very impudent, very ambitious and a complete hypocrite. He walked about the streets with his neck bent, wearing a filthy tattered old robe, and became so popular with the mob that he was followed about everywhere. He knew Italian perfectly and delivered his sermons anywhere, at any time, clutching a crucifix in his hand. In his utter shamelessness he publicly announced that when he was praying at night the angels revealed to him what he was to preach next day. Not content with that he added revelations of his own—saying how one man after death had gone straight to heaven, another had descended into purgatory, while yet another had been plunged into deepest hell, all of which the friar pretended he had by revelation from God. He preached in Calabria with stupendous success; and yet all he did was to denounce sin and reel off anything that came into his head.

About this time it happened that the Catholic king and the wonder of women for all time, his wife Queen Isabella of Castile, ordered the expulsion from Spain of all Jews and Moors. This put into Fra Francisco's head the idea of persuading King Ferdinand to do the same in his kingdom. But King Ferdinand knew that Holy Church permits Jews to dwell among Christians, and he warned the Moors that he would punish any of them who judaized, and paid no attention to what the friar said.

Finding himself treated with contempt, the friar nearly went off his head with rage, preaching against the Jews until he almost succeeded in raising a pogrom, and uttering fearful prophetic threats against both king and people. One day the king sent for him and asked what were his reasons for preaching so bitterly against the Jews. All the friar could think of to say was that they were the generation of vipers who crucified our Redeemer, that they ought to be driven from human society and scattered into deserts, and threatened the king with God's wrath if he failed to imitate his cousin of Spain. Seeing this was all he had to say, the king refused to take him any more seriously than a mountebank or a street-corner orator.

This was more than the conceited, ambitious friar could bear, and in his fanaticism he made up his mind to try other means to make the king expel the Jews. The friar therefore left Naples and went to Taranto, where he had already preached with amazing success. There he secretly got hold of a piece of metal and persuaded another friar—quite an educated man but as wicked as himself—to engrave it with certain words similar to those imprinted by the hand of San Cataldo, a saint greatly revered in those parts. He contrived to bury this piece of metal in an old chapel of San Cataldo, just outside the town; and left it there for three years, while he went up and down the kingdom continually preaching against the Jews.

After three years he returned to Taranto. Although he went about in tatters he had enough money to give a large bribe to the poverty-stricken priest of the chapel, who had about ten pounds a year to live on and eagerly promised to do anything for such a pile of ducats as Fra Francisco offered.

Having dug up the piece of metal, this parish priest went

to Naples and got an audience of the king and made him a long speech. He told the king that he was the poor priest of San Cataldo in Taranto; that the saint had appeared to him in a vision, telling him to dig behind the high altar until he found a certain piece of metal which he was to take to the king; that the king was not to say anything about it until he had consulted the holiest and most famous preacher in the kingdom, and that under penalty of God's wrath the king must do what the holy man advised.

The king listened carefully to what he said and then examined the piece of metal. Although the words engraved on it were enigmatic and obscure they seemed to contain something against the Jews. The good king sat thinking for some time about this matter of expelling the Jews, when suddenly he remembered Fra Francisco and guessed that his finger was in this particular pie. So he turned on the priest half angrily and said:

"Priest! Priest! I'll teach you what it means to make a mock of your prince! This metal is the work of human hands, and I know who made you bring it here. But if you tell me the whole truth, I promise not to harm you."

Master priest knew that the king was not a man to play jokes on and suddenly realized he'd been a great fool to believe in the friar—he could almost feel the hangman's hands at his neck. So he fell at the king's feet, humbly begging for mercy, and told him the whole story, including how the friar had promised he should be a bishop. Finally the king said:

"Sir priest, I pardon you. Enjoy in peace the money the friar gave you and get more out of him if you can. But if you hold life dear listen to what I say and obey me. Return to Taranto and tell the friar that you gave me the piece of metal and that you said to me exactly what he told you to say. Say I listened carefully and declared I didn't believe in these visions. But beware of letting him know that you revealed the secret to me."

ARTIFEX: SKETCHES AND IDEAS

The priest felt as if he had been brought back from death to life and promised the king exact obedience. Off he went to Taranto and told the friar exactly what the king had told him to say. When Master Friar heard this and moreover became certain a few days later that the king did not intend to send for him, he nearly went out of his mind with fury that the king should hold him so cheap and that his wonderful scheme had failed.

Thereafter in every sermon he preached he abused the king. There were new visions and pretended revelations, and he talked so much about the miraculous piece of metal that at last the Pope heard about it and wrote to the king to make enquiries. The king had behaved very cautiously hitherto and had been unwilling to take any action out of respect for the honour of the friars; but now he immediately arrested two of Fra Francisco's closest friends, and they speedily confessed the friar's many crimes. With this confession in writing the king sent them to the Pope, along with the priest who had brought him the piece of metal and Fra Francisco as well. The Pope had the whole matter carefully investigated and discovered they were all adulterous sacrilegious, and possessed of unlawful wealth. He condemned them to prison for life and to fast three times a week on bread and water, and handed them over to the general of their order to purge their sins thus bitterly for the rest of their lives.

Thus ended the visions of Fra Francisco, the Spaniard.

Merely an Egg

Merely an Egg

UNLESS you have lived among the Latin peasants of the last generation you cannot have experienced their peculiar reverence for bread and wine, the traditional basis of their lives. This reverence extends to other kinds of food, so that there is a mystic significance in the family meal to which we in the North are not accustomed. The "grace" we said as children was a conventional thing. In the prosperous class the daily presence of food is taken for granted, and the industrialized workers of towns are so cut off from the realities of the earth that food is merely what you buy in shops and not a great possession won from the mystic Earth Powers by toil and a certain amount of artful magic.

It is—or rather was, for I think it is all changed now—quite otherwise in Italy. I gradually realized this when I was wandering about Italy before the war. As I was very poor I had to eat in wine-shops and small trattorie, among peasants or townspeople so close to peasant life that they had kept most of their traditions. This didn't mean that the eating was genteel and solemn, which is the English idea of reverence. On the contrary it was often noisy and mirthful, with fearful sucking and gulching noises particularly in the soup or spaghetti stages, very harrowing to a youth still not free from public school preju-

ARTIFEX: SKETCHES AND IDEAS

dices. But vaguely I did catch something of this warm reverence, and wondered about it.

Today I should explain it as being religious in origin. At that time religion meant for me the dull chilly feeble Protestant idealism which I had instinctively rejected at fifteen. So far as I was concerned my instructors over-reached themselves by their arrogant assumption that religion was equivalent to their particular brand of Christianity. I now think that Christianity is not a very religious religion, and I know that religion is something far more primitive and ancient and that it would tranquilly survive the total disappearance of Christianity.

So much of Christian mythology—in the South at any rate—is similar to the older myths that the change does not greatly affect the peasants. It doesn't matter to them that the name of the wine and corn god is changed from Bacchus to Jesus, so long as they have a wine and corn god. They had to struggle with dumb obstinacy to get back their Divine Mother, but in the end they got her. The new ethics made little difference to their lives, and the new idealism made no impression on them. Life was still an abominable struggle with the elementary powers which had somehow to be bribed or outwitted. Ever since Ulysses the Southerner has had great fun outwitting the gods. But underneath it all persists this queer dumb reverence for the "powers" and the good essential things of life they give. Long, long ago the heretical Pharaoh said the Sun-god was a beneficent father; and still when the peasant goes to church and looks up at the sacred pictures he is likely to see the Beneficent Father sending out golden rays. The peasant knows very well that the Sun-father isn't always beneficent, but he hopes the picture will give a strong hint as to how He should behave.

I had been in Italy nearly three months when I realized the sacredness of this ancient food ritual very vividly by seeing a breach of it. The woman plays an important part in what I am

MERELY AN EGG

tempted to call this sacred drama of eating. It is the man's duty to earn the food, but as soon as it comes to the house it belongs to the woman. She dresses it, she serves it, and the men never question her serving; they accept what she gives, it is her sacred right. But she is not mistress of the wine. That always belongs to the man. If a peasant invites you to his house, he puts wine before you. All the males present will receive wine, but not the women. And even at meals the man usually pours wine for the woman. It is already bourgeois and improper for the woman to help herself.

I was in Naples and it was rather cold. To prolong my stay I economized by eating bread and oranges for lunch, and having one hot meal at night at a tiny trattoria which had no name except a sign which said Cucina Borghese. It was a humble little place, with only seven or eight tables, and lived chiefly by sending out food to middle-class families in the neighbourhood. To me it seemed very good food and very cheap—and it was far better than I have ever had in Naples since at ten times the money. The people who ate there were mostly poorer commercial travellers and peasants who were passing through Naples.

One night a strange couple arrived. The woman was dressed in rather shabby black, and seemed oddly cowed, humble and frightened, very different from the usual Italian wife who knows she is queen in her own tiny world however much she submits to the man. I noticed that at once as they sat waiting for their meal. For some reason she was afraid of the man, abjectly afraid; and of course the Italians with their intense awareness of other people felt it more than I did. At once there was a different "feel" in the place. Without seeming to, we were all watching, and the nice friendliness of every one was a little alert and suspicious.

The man repelled me at once. He had a dark coarse face and was self-conscious, ostentatious. He was flashily dressed—

ARTIFEX: SKETCHES AND IDEAS

much more expensively than the woman—and his fat ugly hands were covered with imitation rings in the Neapolitan style. I now know that he was what the Italians call an Americano—a peasant who had gone to America and made money. God knows what those peasants suffer in America, but something dreadful happens to them. It is a medical fact that Italian peasant women in America are so unhappy, so utterly soul-destroyed and body-destroyed by the brutality of America, that the first child they bear in the country is frequently an idiot. The men must also suffer. They lose their European soul and America cannot give them another. They lose their old virtues and acquire new vices, brutality and cynicism among them. They pick up the crude cult of a devil-god—dollars. They come back with their new dollar-god, conceited and overbearing; but when they've swanked a little and had a splash, life goes sour to them. The Signoria won't have them; their old companions dislike and mistrust them. So all they can do is to form little groups of Americani, and talk about dollars, and despise the old life. And in time they have gradually infected the whole country. Lire, lire, lire.

Well, we watched the Americano and his woman, as we ate our spaghetti and drank our black Calabrian wine—good wine it was, but too strong, needing a lot of water. The Americano drank his wine neat, as Americani do. Spaghetti wasn't good enough; and we others already disliked him so much that we were offended at his ordering beefsteak and fried potatoes, as if he were a real Yankee and not just an Americano. When at last a pile of thin fried slices of meat and a huge mound of potatoes were set before the woman there seemed to be a chuckle in the air at the fool Americano. *We* knew the biftecchi would be tough.

And then suddenly the good humour vanished almost with a snap, and a thrill of sacred horror and indignation went through the little whitewashed room. Every one bristled. Even

MERELY AN EGG

the frightful moustache of the oleograph King Victor Emmanuel would have bristled if it had been possible. The Americano roughly pulled the dish away from the woman and prepared to help the food, thereby depriving her of her essential queen-woman right in her own microcosm. At that moment I noticed for the first time, with a pang, that she was only allowed water to drink. Another bitter slight.

The Americano helped—himself first. He piled his plate high with potatoes and most of the meat, and then gave her the scanty leavings. He spoke to her in a rough loud voice—something I didn't catch—and she murmured a reply, her head bowed in a kind of dreadful submission and humiliation. Perhaps you may think all this a little fanciful and imagined, but there could be no doubt of her humiliation and frightened pathetic subjection. All her shabby body spoke humiliation, and the hopeless bend of her neck—as if she could never raise it and look the world frankly and fearlessly in the eyes—somehow smote to my heart with another sharper pang of pity and sorrow. It was the first time that my arrogant young manhood was pierced with the knowledge of the long dumb suffering of women. Her life had gone dead and hopeless. She knew how he bullied and humiliated her, but for some reason I could not then guess she was bound to him, she could never leave him. If she had ever hoped to get free from him, she would never have submitted and humiliated herself before him with such hopeless pathetic patience, like an ill-treated bitch.

What was their story? What was behind it? Perhaps you know that Italy better than I, and can guess. For me they were peasants, both from the Abruzzi. When they were quite young they had fallen in love, in that Italian way which is physically so real and intense, and so completely false and ridiculous in its sentimental verbiage when it tries to express itself in words. Nothing is more idiotic and apparently insincere than an Italian love letter—they use all the mouldiest clichés of the deadest of

ARTIFEX: SKETCHES AND IDEAS

dead romanticism à la Verdi; and nothing is more genuine than their physical passion.

These two, I thought, were very poor then, so poor they could not marry even as peasants. So he said he would go to America and make money for them, and he would come back rich and they would be married and live like Signoria. And they plighted their troth, and he went away. I can imagine the heavy black grief of their souls when they parted, the awful Italian melancholy which would turn his face green-yellow and leave her sitting hunched up like a sack of grain flung on a bench, her eyes streaming with hopeless tears.

Maybe they corresponded, but probably neither could read, and their halting dictated letters embellished with the frightful sentimentality of the professional letter writers, instead of keeping up the bond between them, merely bewildered them, showed up the gap of absence. These words were not their words, and in any case they hadn't been accustomed to communicate much with words, but in a dumb physical way. All Italians are always talking, except lovers. The lovers sit together, in a dreamy silence, lost in a swoon of bodily communion. So the letters were useless.

Then there was the change in Giuseppe, which he could never have explained to Maria, even if he had been able to talk to her across the Atlantic. The only way for them to keep together in the change would have been for her to go dumbly through the same experience and change with him. But she didn't, she was in Italy and he was in America, suffering terribly at first, and then with Italian courage and pertinacity adapting to the brutal circumstances by becoming a brute. Perhaps something of this got into the letters, always bragging of dollars and American conveniences, those infernal conveniences which are death to the old peasant life. And perhaps, feeling that and being tempted in the man's absence as women are, Maria took another lover. Then suddenly Giuseppe turned up, dollar-rich

MERELY AN EGG

and life-poor, an Americano bragging and arrogant, making up for all the fearful humiliations in America by domineering in Italy with his money. Getting his own back.

And since marrying Maria was part of the scheme for getting his own back, marry her he must, bribing and dazzling the old parents with the fiendish dollars. But of course he knew about the other man. . . .

But—you may well ask!—what has all this to do with the "mere egg" of my title? Indeed, it is a monstrous prologue to an egg and butter, but it seemed necessary in order to explain why an apparently very trivial incident made an impression on me so deep that I remember it clearly after a good many years. . . .

I did not return to Italy until the late summer of 1922. That to me was a very beautiful time, a period of real healing of the inner war wounds. I seem to have forgotten nearly all the unpleasant things—they must surely have existed—and to remember only what was pleasant and lovely.

How many Northerners, I wonder, remember the extraordinary wines of that year? In Italy the wine drunk is nearly all from the vintage of the previous year, and 1921 was a glorious year, a superb parting gift from the old gods to the old Italy which is no more. Those wines of the Roman castelli! Especially the white ones, so delicate and fragrant, liquid sunlight, running through a whole series of golds and yellows from the pale straw colour of Trebbiano to the rich orange glow of Frascati. Every little wine-shop poured nectar in one's glass, and vine-wreathed Bacchus was the god of Rome in those sunny weeks. I remember reading the *Bacchus in Tuscany* of Redi over a flask of cooled Trebbiano, and feeling the ecstasy of the god:

"*Montepulciano d'ogni vino é il re!*"

As a matter of fact, Montepulciano is a heavy red wine, cloying and alcoholic, not to be compared with the fine (finissimi!) white wines of Rome.

ARTIFEX: SKETCHES AND IDEAS

Before going to Rome that year, I spent a week in Florence; and that too was a revelation. The first week in September was terrifically hot—I nearly fainted in the close over-heated air of the unventilated Uffizi—and there were practically no foreigners. Florence, for once, belonged entirely to the Florentines. I used to sit at a little café near the Duomo to watch the endless sauntering crowds. The men were mostly in white or alpaca summer suits, and the women in very thin brightly coloured dresses with flower patterns. How very charming those Florentine girls were, passing in groups of three and four, chattering like mad, and showing off their lithe girl bodies so gaily and impudently! They, with their dark braided hair and proud elastic backs, they knew they were fresh and desirable and that the men were looking at them. If Bacchus was king of Rome that year, Venus was queen of Florence. It is the only time I have ever thought Italian women in the mass really beautiful. I felt it a great honour to be allowed just to look at them, and to hear real young laughter again after all the grim misery and hideous cocktail gaiety of the North. . . .

The only people I knew in Florence at that moment were the Mortons. He was an Englishman of good family, supposed to be a painter, and had lived in Italy for years. Somehow he had managed to dodge the war, but had spent his money, and had to scratch a living by his art—a difficult matter enough, even if he hadn't been as lazy as a half-wakened dormouse. Not that he was dull—on the contrary a devilish lively fellow so long as no work was involved. He had been handsome, but was running to seed with too much far niente which can't have been particularly dolce.

I think this shows the kind of fellow Morton was. . . . He came to see me about eleven on my first morning, and after about an hour's very gay talk we went and drank iced lemonade at the café near the Signoria. I suggested he lunch with me, and after a little hesitation he accepted, and we had a really splendid time, incidentally doing for the best part of a flask of delicious white wine from the Val d'Arno. After two years of continuous hard work, the holiday seemed to bring me alive. We didn't separate until nearly four. Afterwards I found that he had missed an appointment which would have brought him some of the work he needed so badly and hated doing so much. And he could easily have kept his appointment and rejoined me for lunch; but that was too much trouble in the heat.

Mrs. Morton was Italian and they had one child, a turbulent little brat of a boy about five. He was like his mother and therefore very good-looking. It used to hurt me to see her patiently endure the child's really disgusting temper and roughness. I have seen the child kick her savagely, or jump on her lap with dusty shoes and hit and hit at her face in one of his nasty rages. He must have hurt her, but she gently put him from her with a sweet hurt smile, really like a Madonna. Morton had taste and knew a good deal about women. He showed that by his choice of a wife. She was that rare Tuscan type, with the delicate oval face, soft hair and large blue-grey eyes of the Botticelli women; but instead of their languor she still retained a certain energy and health. Only the slight coarseness of hands and feet showed a peasant strain in her, but I mustn't blame hands which had grown coarse through working for Morton and that beastly child.

They were very poor, but they still had a couple of nice rooms on the Pitti side of the river, with a loggia looking over Florence. The furniture was old stuff saved from the wreck, some of it very handsome; and they still had quite good clothes. In the big cool living-room, with the Florentine chests and the view through the open loggia, they didn't look poor—upper-class Bohemia you would have said, as I said to myself.

The day before I left for Rome I went to see them after lunch by invitation. I had dropped into the Florentine early

ARTIFEX: SKETCHES AND IDEAS

lunch, and when I arrived the Mortons had only just finished their spaghetti. Of course, they wouldn't let me go, and I sat at the wide loggia window looking back into the room and talking to Morton. I noticed with surprise that they were not drinking wine. Presently Mrs. Morton came in from the kitchen with the remainder of the meal.

It was meagre—a couple of eggs and some bread and butter. She put one egg and most of the bread and butter before her husband, and began to feed the child with the other egg. I watched the child with some distaste—he was kicking up his legs, making uncouth noises and kept trying to knock out of her hand the spoonful of egg she patiently held out to him. She ate nothing herself.

Afflicted with matrimonial blindness and deafness, Morton perceived nothing of this. He soon polished off his egg and bread and butter, talking away quite unaware of my growing embarrassment—for one second Mrs. Morton's eye had met mine and I could see in her cheek a faint flush of shame, shame on his account I like to think. Presently Morton turned to her and began grumbling in Italian. Did she think this was a proper meal to give a man? What was she thinking about? Why was she such a rotten housekeeper? Perché? Perché? He knew jolly well. In her silly Italian way she forgot all about the husband as soon as she had the child. Bringing up the child against his father. And keeping all the food for herself and the child in the mean sneaky Italian way. Perché? Why did she do it? Perché? Perché?

There was something inexpressibly harsh and beastly in his voice. I hated him. I hated his injustice. Couldn't the fool see she was starving herself to feed him and his brat? And there he was glowering at her, and hammering on her nerves—and incidentally on mine—with that stupid raging "Perché? Perché? Why? Why?" If it hurt me almost beyond endurance, how must it have hurt her who loved him? And there she sat

MERELY AN EGG

motionless and speechless, with her beautiful head bowed humbly before him, a real Madonna dolorosa, and he stuck sword after sword in her heart. I wanted to hit him....

Suddenly the worst pang of all came to me. I remembered. The humiliated body, the humble bent neck, the submission to the male domineering and brutality—it was exactly the same as that poor peasant woman years before in Naples. But this woman was a lady and beautiful like a Madonna, and the brute was not an Americano, but an English gentleman, one of the fine English gentlemen she had heard of in her girlhood, the rich English gentlemen who think nothing too good for their wives and always treat them delicately like queens, never in the arrogant Italian way. And there she was, that Madonna, humbly bowed before her English milord, exactly as the peasant woman had bowed in humility before her coarse Americano....

I got up and walked to the end of the loggia. I almost wanted to walk over the edge of it and drop the fifty feet to the pavement below. Instead, I stood there blinking in the bright sunlight, trying to make out the red roofs and towers of Florence, the Lily City which only the English and the Americani are now sensitive enough to understand and love.

The Jubilee

The Jubilee

THE following account of a great procession held at Alexandria in the reign of Ptolemy Philadelphus comes from a book on Alexandria written in the third century B.C. by one Callixeinus of Rhodes. Unluckily his works have disappeared, and this long fragment has survived only because it was quoted by Athenaeus in that enormous and amusing rag-bag of citations, the Deipnosophistae. Athenaeus was a Greek of Naucratis in Egypt and wrote in the early part of the third century A.D. He spent his life in Rome, and it is only too obvious that his taste was corrupted by Roman vulgarity. He admits that he quotes from Callixeinus chiefly those passages which display the wealth of Alexandria. The question of taste and of the motives for this remarkable exhibition has no interest for him. Already here one feels the approaching penumbra of medieval incuriosity and stupidity, the spirit of "Oo-er!" which only wants to be astonished and cares nothing for experience and understanding.

It must be admitted that even the earlier writer seems to have been obsessed by ideas of costliness and size. Indeed I should imagine that he did not see the pageant he describes, but merely reproduced the Treasury officials' check list of valuable objects loaned from the royal treasury and combined it with the official programme. He or Athenaeus entirely omits

ARTIFEX: SKETCHES AND IDEAS

to tell us how so stupendous a procession was organized, how in this all-day affair it was fed and provided with comfort stations, how if the pageant lasted all day there was time for "games" and a banquet, and why it was held at all. Neither does he tell us how it was policed and how this immense treasure was protected from the enterprise of thieves, for the army apparently did not line the routes, but followed in the rear. Nor does he tell us how tender maidens managed to carry large weights of gold, though admittedly women show great heroism under such burdens.

The ancient Pharaohs were accustomed to hold "jubilees" very frequently—they are recorded on the famous Palermo stone. I assume that the Egyptianized Ptolemies adopted this custom. Possibly the festivity was associated with the very ancient religious displays in honour of Osiris. It will be noticed that Dionysus plays a large part in the pageant. The Greeks identified Osiris with Dionysus, and as Pharaoh, Ptolemy himself would be identified with Osiris. The ancient trinity of Osiris, Isis and Horus seems here to have dropped into the background, and instead of the great mystery play of the life, death and resurrection of Osiris there were athletic games. These Greek Pharaohs evidently altered the ancient religion to suit their own purposes, and already we see the ancient mysteries degraded to flatter the man as a god and not as of old to reverence the godlike symbol in the man.

But let us come to the procession.

We are told that the pageant "took place" in the great stadium at Alexandria; but evidently no stadium could be large enough to hold more than a fraction of such a vast concourse at one time. We must imagine that the Pharaoh, such of his officers as were not on duty, the women, and privileged classes sat in the stadium to watch the pageant go by. The "strangers" mentioned also probably had seats if they could pay for them, though nothing is said about payment. The rest of Egypt and

THE JUBILEE

the visitors would line the road leading to and from the stadium.

The show began at dawn, and the first part of the procession was dedicated to the Morning Star. The last section was named for the Evening Star, and in between came sections dedicated to Ptolemy Soter and Berenice, and others "named after all the gods." We are not told which gods, and the historian immediately proceeds to describe the procession of Dionysus, which evidently he considered most important. Premising that he tends to wander and to mix up one part of the pageant with another, I offer an "order of the pageant." If, instead of glancing hastily through it in the manner of the modern cinema-minded reader, you read it slowly and try to imagine what it looked like, you may get something out of it.

ORDER OF THE PAGEANT

Sileni in red or purple riding-cloaks, keeping back the crowds.

Twenty Satyrs who remained at each entrance to the stadium. They carried torches twined with gilt ivy-leaves.

Women dressed as Victories, wearing embroidered tunics and heavy gold jewellery; they had gold wings and carried censers nine (?) feet high wreathed with gilt ivy.

The Car of the Double Altar. This altar was nine feet long and carved with gilt ivy in high relief; a crown of gold vine-leaves rested on it.

120 boys in purple, carrying gold vessels of frankincense, myrrh and saffron.

Forty naked Satyrs, whose bodies were stained purple or vermilion, with ivy crowns of gold.

Two Sileni in purple with white shoes, one bearing a trumpet, one a herald's staff, in gold.

Between them "The Year," a man of great stature dressed as a tragic actor and carrying a gold cornucopia.

The Lustrum, or period of Four Years, a very beautiful tall woman, heavily laden with gold. She carried a palm branch and a wreath of Egyptian leaves.

The Four Seasons, "appropriately dressed" and carrying fruits.

ARTIFEX: SKETCHES AND IDEAS

Two large gold censers wreathed with ivy and a gold altar.

Red-garbed Satyrs with gold ivy-crowns, carrying gold cups and wine-jars.

The poet Philiscus, priest of Dionysus, followed by the company of actors of Dionysus.

Delphic tripods, the prizes for the trainers in the games.

The Car of Dionysus, drawn by 180 men. The canopy was decorated with ivy, vine-tendrils and fruits, wreaths, ribbons, thyrsus rods, tambourines, and masks of Tragedy, Comedy and Satiric Drama. In front of the car was a huge gold mixing-bowl, and a tripod holding a gold censer and two gold vessels of cassia and saffron. The statue of Dionysus was clad in purple and saffron robes, and held a gold cup for libations.

The priests and priestesses of Dionysus, and women carrying the sacred fans.

Bacchantes, with loose hair, and wreaths of snakes or ivy or vine or smilax, carrying snakes or daggers.

The Car of Nysa, drawn by 60 men. There was a canopy, and gold-banded torches at each corner of the car. The statue had a crown of gold ivy-leaves and jewelled grape-clusters; it was draped in yellow and gold and carried a thyrsus rod. By some concealed and undescribed mechanism this statue was made to rise up, pour a libation of milk from a gold cup, and then sit down. It is not stated at what intervals.

Car of the Wine Press, drawn by 300 men. To the music of pipes and under the command of Silenus, 60 Satyrs were treading grapes in an enormous wine-press, so that the must ran over.

Car of the Wine Skin, drawn by 600 men. Thirty thousand gallons of wine were carried in an enormous "skin" made of leopard-skins joined together. The wine slowly trickled out as the car moved.

120 Sileni and Satyrs, carrying gold wine-jugs and cups.

Car of the Silver Wine Bowl, drawn by 600 men. The bowl was of solid silver, decorated with "figures," jewelled and banded with a gold wreath. Its capacity was six thousand gallons.

Smaller Cars of the Silver Vessels, two chased stands 18 feet high, 10 bowls of 300 gallons, 16 bowls of 50 gallons, silver cauldrons, wine-presses, tripods, water-jars, amphoras and wine-coolers. One of the tripods had a circumference of 24 feet. There was a table of solid silver 18 feet long, and 30 solid silver tables 9 feet long. The total of these silver objects amounted to 393. Most of them were large.

Smaller Cars of the Gold Vessels, of similar kind, but including a sort of

THE JUBILEE

buffet of gold covered with gold vessels of various kinds. The exact numbers are not given, but they were numerous.

1600 boys in white tunics, crowned with pine or ivy, carrying 250 gold jugs, 400 silver jugs, 350 gold or silver wine-coolers. 370 boys carried 20 gold jars, 50 silver jars and 300 painted jars, and scattered perfumed water on the spectators.

Cars of Statue Groups, only some of which are described. They included:

Car of the Bridal Chamber of Semele, where the statues were dressed in gold tunics with many jewels.

Car of the Cave of the Child Dionysus, drawn by 500 men. Hermes with a staff of gold and Nymphs with gold crowns stood beside the Holy Child at the entrance to a cave shaded with yew and ivy. Two fountains played, one of milk and one of wine. All along the way doves and pigeons were let loose from the cavern, and they had strings attached to them so that they could be caught by the people.

Car of the Return of Dionysus from India. The elephant carrying the god had gold trappings, and the mahout was a Satyr wearing a pine-wreath of gold and waving a gold horn. Dionysus carried a gold thyrsus; he wore a purple cloak and wreath of ivy and vine of gold.

500 girls in purple with gold girdles, 120 of whom wore gold pine-wreaths.

120 Satyrs, armed in gold or silver or bronze.

Sileni and Satyrs wearing crowns and mounted on donkeys, with gold and silver harness.

24 elephants drawing cars.
60 teams of goats.
12 of ?.
7 of gazelles.
15 of hartbeestes (?).
8 of ostriches.
7 of antelopes.
4 of wild asses.
4 four-horsed chariots.

These animals were for the children, the little boys driving and wearing pine crowns or charioteers' hats, the little girls standing beside them carrying shields and thyrsus rods, in gold-threaded dresses.

ARTIFEX: SKETCHES AND IDEAS

6 teams of camels.

Mule-carts with tents, showing Indian and other foreign women.

Camels bearing frankincense, myrrh, saffron cassia, cinnamon, orris-root and other spices in large quantities.

Negroes, carrying 600 tusks of ivory, 2000 pieces of ebony wood and sixty bowls full of gold dust and gold and silver coins.

Two hunters carrying gilt spears.

2400 dogs of all kinds, including those of India, Hyrcania and Molossos.

150 men carrying branches with "all kinds of animals and birds."

Cages of parrots, peacocks, guinea-hens, pheasants and Aethiopian birds in large numbers.

130 Aethiopian sheep.

300 Arabian sheep.

20 Euboean sheep.

26 pure white oxen from India.

8 Aethiopian oxen.

1 large white she-bear (? a polar bear).

14 leopards.

16 panthers.

4 lynxes.

3 panther cubs.

1 giraffe.

1 rhinoceros.

Car of Dionysus. He was represented at the Altar of Rhea, taking refuge from Hera. Priapus was with him. All had gold wreaths or crowns.

Car of Alexander and Ptolemy, wearing gold ivy-crowns, and accompanied by Virtue with a gold crown of olives, Priapus with a gold ivy-wreath, Corinth with a gold fillet. Besides them was a 50 gallon gold bowl and a stand of gold cups.

Car of the Greek cities—women in rich garments wearing gold crowns.

Car of the Golden Thyrsus Rod, 135 feet long.

Car of the Silver Spear, 90 feet long.

Car of the Gold Phallus and Star, 180 feet long.

Here comes a break in the narrative. Athenaeus says that hitherto he has only mentioned those sections of the procession

THE JUBILEE

which included gold and silver objects. He speaks of "large numbers of wild animals and horses," including 24 lions. Then resumes quotation:

> Cars with statues of the gods and kings.
> A choral orchestra of 600 men, of whom 300 had gilded harps and gold crowns.
> 2000 bulls, all of the same colour. Their horns were gilt and wreathed with gold, they had gold stars on their foreheads and gold chains and plectrums.

Already the obsession with gold and silver has returned, and the narrative now becomes a confused list of all kinds of monstrously big objects in gold, which arouse serious suspicions that somebody was drawing the long-bow. Apparently the pageant of Dionysus was followed by one of Zeus and one of the other gods "in great number." Last came the pageant of Alexander. His chariot was drawn by elephants, and his gold statue stood in the chariot between Athena and Victory. The gold or gilded objects included palm trees, tripods, braziers, altars, "a thunder-bolt 60 feet long," a temple, animals and eagles "30 feet high!" And so he goes on, from his 3200 gold crowns down to his 20 carts of gold vessels, 400 of silver and 800 of spices.

The 23,000 cavalry and 57,000 infantry of the Royal army which wound up the affair must have seemed an anti-climax. But there was still the royal banquet for the 100 chosen, given in a hall specially built for the occasion, decorated in scarlet and white with hanging tapestries, purple curtains, skins of animals, 100 statues by great artists, paintings, embroidered robes, shields of gold and silver, statue-groups of drinking parties and scenes from Tragedy, Comedy and the Satyric plays, with gold eagles at the roof and gold sphinx couches on the floor. There were Persian carpets to walk on, and "flowers in profusion" etcetera. How the gastronomic Athenaeus came to omit the menu is a mystery, but we need not regret it.

I do not wish to be ungrateful to my authors, but between them they have made a nice hash of this remarkable affair. It begins with a detail which enables one to visualize the pageant very well. Then one or both of them got bored, and instead of continuing the description went in for an orgiastic inventory of expensive objects. A pity—I should have liked the whole pageant.

But what of the pageant itself? Obviously, the most interesting question to the modern reader will be: Were the gold and silver real? I should say, undoubtedly. The narrative is careful to distinguish between "gold" and "gilt." If the size of the objects is considered exorbitant—and there was plenty of chance for exaggeration and miscopying—I should say the answer is that these large things were not solid, but either thinly beaten gold or sheets of gold fastened on to wood. But I think the gold and silver were real—the mania for "acceptable substitutes" had not yet smitten an unscientific world.

This Ptolemy must have been rich. The little entertainment cost over 700,000 gold pounds, which was instantaneously subscribed by his delighted subjects in the stadium, who also voted him a gold crown and statue. I suggest that the gold and silver carried in procession were simply part of the metal reserves of the State. But instead of keeping them all in squalid ingots locked up in the bowels of the earth, as our masters now do, Ptolemy very sensibly had them made into things he could use and look at, and in the goodness of his royal heart desired that his loving people might look upon them too. Clearly his taste was far from good, and under him the ancient mysteries had degenerated into a plutocratic Lord Mayor's Show on a grand scale. But these Macedonians were barbarians, powerless to stimulate creativeness in literature and the arts. All they

THE JUBILEE

could do was to found a university, which has since become a universally "accepted substitute" for a living culture.

Processions seem to satisfy a very ancient and profound need in human psychology. They are one of the numerous human necessities which economists generally overlook. Power-wielders have always made use of them, but if the power-wielders forget them or want them all to themselves (as in England) the people are apt to arrange them on their own. I once saw in London, on the Embankment, part of a huge and entirely uninteresting procession of post-office workers, carrying banners inscribed with horrid threats against the "threat" to their wages. Needless to say, their wages were cut as the Government had determined, but the post-office people had the fun of their procession. I only wish it had been more fun for them. Similarly with the May-day processions which agitate earnest-minded people and bother the police. So long as there are flags to wave and songs to sing, most of them care nothing really which flag and which songs. Only, if they are not given legitimate purposes for processions, they naturally are driven to seditious ones.

In the United States "monster" processions are a familiar spectacle. They are extremely tasteless and noisy, but appear to give general satisfaction. They do these things better in Russia and Germany, where positively enormous crowds are marched and massed in melodramatic formations and then subjected to inflammatory harangues. Similarly in Italy, where the quasi-comical spectacle may be enjoyed of the Head of the State leading a procession of cars down a new street or over a new bridge. Looked at coolly from the outside all these modern developments of the "procession spirit" seem comical. But be sure that those who take part in them are in deadly earnest. They wouldn't be fun if they weren't believed to be somehow important and mysteriously effective. How? I don't

ARTIFEX: SKETCHES AND IDEAS

know. Does anybody? The ethnologists, archeologists and psychologists must settle it between them.

I have already made one or two suggestions as to the purpose of Ptolemy's procession. But whatever the purpose, I should say that it achieved its real aim of giving a good time to all. Observe that the army was not allowed to hog the whole thing, but only came in at the rear, probably to pick up the drunks and the pieces, and to get the Pharaoh's party safely out of the stadium. Neither did Pharaoh take more than his fair share; he had the fun of going to and from the stadium, but in between sat in his throne like a gentleman and graciously allowed them to parade his statue. Notice how everybody had a share—the children, the boys and maidens, the women and men were all given congenial parts. There was an enormous band for the musical; the comical cards could play their pranks and jokes as Satyrs; the good citizens could toil at dragging the cars; and the revellers trod the wine-press. The women all had splendid dresses and jewels and had to look pretty. The older boys and girls had valuable things to carry. And the children had a regular Zoo outing, driving their little cars behind teams of goats and gazelles and ostriches—I wish I'd been allowed to drive an ostrich team in a procession when I was eight. All I had was gracious permission to watch Lord Curzon be made Lord Warden of the Cinque Ports and he didn't even ride on an elephant—I've always wondered why I disliked that man.

Almost everybody in that crowd at Alexandria must have had a child or a relative in the procession. And certainly every one in the procession knew that somewhere along the route or in the stadium relatives and friends would be looking out for him. Imagine the kudos for Ptolemy, the *tendresse* for his person engendered in the bosoms of the mothers alone as they watched the only child in the procession with his sister, clad in robes from the royal wardrobe, driving pretty (and let us hope,

THE JUBILEE

safely-led) animals from the royal Zoo, in the great royal procession in honour of the gods Dionysus and Ptolemy! Upon my word, I feel quite touched myself. Vive Ptolémée!

Quel bon petit roi
C'était là, là, là!

The Partridge

The Partridge

IN VICTORIAN days this little piece would naturally have borne the sub-title: Or the pursuit of grandeur under difficulties. Nowadays the grand manner and the grand pose are equally out of date in the arts and in society, and it seems remarkable that they can ever have existed. Yet I, who am not so old, have been gratified by witnessing displays of the grand artistic manner by the Authentic Bard, W. B. Yeats, and no less astonishing performances in the grand social manner by Charlie Plantagenet, the Authentic Aristocrat. Although Charlie is dead—I wish he were alive, poor old fellow—I give him an obviously fantastic name to preserve the decencies of anonymity.

I remember the period of meeting him very vividly. It was just after the battle of the Marne, and Marion and I had accepted a week-end invitation to the country, thinking it might calm our emotions after those hectic and unbelievable six weeks.

We arrived about four, and while still vibrating with the nervous excitement of London at war, found ourselves cast into the tumult of a country tea-party. Our hostess was something of a figure in contemporary literature, while her husband —if you could believe him—was considerably ahead of the ideal superman. So we weren't surprised to find ourselves the only representatives of Bohemian Youth in a gathering of the County. The air seemed heavily charged with patriotism and the right thing. I still remember my surprise and chagrin that there was no butler.

The London-bred maid-servant announced:

"Capting Charles Plentegnit."

A tall slim elderly man, dressed in the peace-time uniform of a Staff Officer with prodigiously tight trousers braced under the boots, entered, precipitated himself gracefully towards our hostess, clicked his heels, bowed low and kissed her hand, exclaiming in mincing tones:

"Deah lady!"

Marion and I looked at each other quickly. I saw she was asking herself the same question—is it real? Unscrupulously I tried to listen, but after a few more words the Capting was already off on a tour of the room, bowing, heel-clicking, hand-kissing and "deah ladying" every woman in turn. It was not long before Eva—our hostess—brought him up to Marion.

"Deah lady! How charming!"

I heard Eva's quick perky voice say to Marion:

"He's a *royal* Plantagenet, you know."

And then to Charlie:

"They were at the Slade together—romantic, isn't it?"

"Vewy womantic," said Charlie.

I was absorbed into the group. Charlie didn't kiss my hand or call me "deah laddie," as I almost hoped. He limply waggled his fingers against mine, almost on a level with my nose, and said "Howdedoo?" I couldn't believe it. I thought—as you probably do—that such people only existed in the rickety imagination of Ouida. But it was true, I swear it was.

He seemed to take to us at once. By the affability of his manner, the dignity without a trace of condescension, I was irresistibly reminded of the dix-huitième, the age-long alliance of aristocrat and artist. We were accepted, we had a place in his hierarchy. A little later I was able to observe his freezingly lofty insolence to a wealthy brewer and his lady, who were probably going to "do something" for Eva if she introduced them to the Royal Plantagenet.

Meanwhile Charlie chatted—in good journalese Royalties always "chat." What style did we work in? The modern? Of course, but which precisely? We murmured something about Cézanne and the Omega—it was twenty years ago, remember. Plainly he had never heard of either, but that didn't matter. Did we remember Freddy Leighton and old Millais? Of course not, much too young. He told us with exquisite propriety about Millais and Mrs. Ruskin, as if it were a piece of choice secret gossip and not common historical knowledge.

"Leighton and Millais painted my first Amazon," he said. "In the days when I was dancin attendance on the old Widow. The Jews have got em now, in the natural course of things. Trwyin to the higher feelins."

Only later did we discover that in Charlie's vocabulary "Amazon" stood for "wife," and "widow" for Queen Victoria, or rather Victorwia. When we told Charlie about some of our queer acquaintances in Montmartre, he said they "sounded a wum lot." Then, as it was evidently impolite to give too much royal attention to one couple, he moved away, intimating that he would be "vewy happy" to see more of us.

By this time we were enthusiastic Charlie fans. We had expected to be stifled by Eva's quasi-County connections, and here was a human specimen of undoubted interest—a genuine original, a splendidly preserved fossil of a fantastic old regime. But, being cynical young people, we didn't want to be spoofed. We liked Charlie, but it was important that he should be genuine. It wouldn't be any fun if he turned out to be an adventurer with a manner borrowed from society novelists who had never been known to Society.

ARTIFEX: SKETCHES AND IDEAS

As soon as the room was empty, we descended on Eva with questions. She assured us that Charlie was certainly king of Gothlandia by divine right, though somebody else enjoyed the throne. His family had been so long in England as to become thoroughly anglicized. Certainly he had been in the Army and had been A.D.C. to royalty, though Eva thought he no longer had any legal right to wear the uniform. But how, we asked, had Charlie fallen from his high estate, not as monarch, but as English gentleman?

"Oh," said Eva, "there were matrimonial troubles and a divorce, and then Charlie lost most of his money. He's the kind of innocent who always gets into trouble, and he's always horribly in debt."

When we hinted that Charlie might be a fake after all, Eva wouldn't have it. She had known him in the days of his glory when he had been very kind to her, and that was why she wouldn't drop him in his déchéance. We put it to her that Charlie's mannerisms of speech made the story improbable, but she assured us they were like that in Charlie's set.

"Wum fellows," I suggested.

"Vewy wum," said Eva laughing.

Privately Marion and I lamented that since we were leaving on Monday night we should lose Charlie before we'd had a chance to enjoy him. Here we were mistaken. At a correct hour on Sunday, Charlie turned up, and asked us if we wouldn't like to visit "a herwo fwom Mons" who was lying wounded in the village. We said we should be delighted, and set out.

Charlie chatted gaily and amusingly as we followed a winding lane. This time it was not his manner which astonished us but his extreme ignorance of what we had learned to think were the realities of our time. It was like listening to the political views of the Duc de Saint-Simon. Some idea of Charlie's views may be learned from the fact that he seemed to think

THE PARTRIDGE

the Lord Chamberlain was politically more important than the Prime Minister ("a wotten wadical"), and that he assured us the war arose out of the insolence of the German Emperor to the King Emperor by not dipping his pennant when his yacht came into the Solent. I couldn't help wondering whether Charlie was trying to pull our legs.

We found the "herwo" in a large feather bed which occupied most of a very stuffy room. With some difficulty we and various members of the family crowded in, and stood at the foot of the bed. I can't remember what Charlie said, but it was admirable—exactly the right thing from one of the High Command visiting the wounded. But the spoiled "herwo" was not in the least grateful or impressed. As the one genuine representative of our heroic little Army in the village he had received much adulation, while frequent rehearsal had made him perfect in his tale. His account of sturdy resolution in the face of fearful odds and horrors would have done credit to a sensational war correspondent, though in justice to the "herwo" I'm bound to admit he said nothing about angels.

To my surprise Charlie was not in the least taken in by this highly coloured tale. When the "herwo" said:

"An at night when I tries to get a bit o sleep I sees them there Zepplins a-circling round and round, and ears the bombs a-crashin all round me...."

Charlie whispered to me:

"Been celebwatin victorwy and herwoism too fweely in the flowin cups."

Charlie escorted us back to Eva's, and at the gate invited us to dine with him that evening. To our genuine regret we had to refuse. Marion explained that Eva was taking us to dine with a Mrs. Cope-Witherington. We gladly arranged to lunch with him on Monday, but were surprised when he asked eagerly if we couldn't bring Mrs. Cope-Witherington and "intrwoduce her" to him. We had to tell him we'd never seen the lady, that she was a friend of Eva's and that we couldn't presume on so slight an acquaintance to carry an invitation. At this Charlie sighed and looked sad, but went off cheerily enough, exaggerating his cavalry walk.

Eva cleared this up for us. Mrs. Witherington was a young member of a "set" which had dropped Charlie long ago, and presumably he had for a moment nourished the pathetic hope of getting back to it through us and her. Eva was hard-hearted about it, but we felt sorry for Charlie. How much he must have suffered from his ostracism if he could grasp so eagerly at the straw of two social nobodies like ourselves in the impossible hope of "getting back!"

Charlie's palace was a ten-room villa of red brick with pleasant views over the sea. The garden looked extremely neat, and clean sand had been freshly spread on the short drive. From a white flag-staff in the garden fluttered the royal banner of Gothlandia—his majesty was at home. A sulky-looking man-servant, whose appearance suggested both batman and gardener and whose manner indicated that answering the door was not his duty, rather unceremoniously brought us to the room where Charlie was waiting.

Here again we were surprised. Hints from Eva and the royal banner in the garden had led us to expect that Charlie might throw his royal weight about. On the contrary. He couldn't have been more charming if we had been exiled royalties. True, he spoiled the effect by premature inquiries about Mrs. Cope-Witherington, but we let that pass.

The room itself was a surprise. The look of the house outside suggested furnishings of sham antique tempered by sporting relics. But no, we found ourselves in a roomful of magnificent and genuine antiques arranged as tastefully as a modern Italian museum. There was not a trace of the *style pompier* which has

THE PARTRIDGE

been adopted as obligatory by reigning houses. Seeing our interest and appreciation, Charlie at once began showing his relics of grandeur without a shadow of boasting or ostentation.

We were allowed to handle Renaissance statuettes, first-class ivories, exquisite eighteenth-century fans and snuff-boxes, miniatures of Charlie's orbed and sceptered ancestors. He opened a safe cunningly built into the wall and amazed us by producing gold plate and goblets chased with the arms of Gothlandia and fine old jewels in worn red morocco cases embossed with the same arms. Marion knows far more about such things than I do, and I saw from her manner of touching them that they were genuine. She told me afterwards that they were worth many thousands of pounds.

Charlie had been frivolous about his objects of *vertu*, but he grew solemn over this valuable flotsam of a lost throne.

"They're a sacwed twust," he explained impressively. "They belong to The Family. They all go to my boy when I cwoke."

We didn't know what to say. It was the first and only time we ever saw Charlie take himself and his doubtless unmerited misfortunes with anything but gay frivolity. Luckily the servant came to announce luncheon, and we helped Charlie lock the jewels away. I liked to think of his being loyal to his "sacwed twust" when from all we'd heard he was so devilish hard up. I have a romantic admiration for senseless and unprofitable loyalties.

Lunch was served in a small summer house in the garden. It was really delightful, and Charlie exerted himself to amuse and please us. He told us a lot about his two "Amazons," how "the Widow lent us a cottage at Kew when my first Amazon kittened"—a nice way of calling the lady a cat, I thought—and "how my second Amazon made herself widiculous, wan away with a gwoom, and wepented it."

In those days I paid little attention to food, but even then the lunch seemed to me a little frugal. We drank our water—there was no wine—from beautiful old goblets, and the little there was to eat came to us on regal plates. The only course which could remotely be called substantial was partridge, a portion of which was served to each of us. By this time Charlie was in great good humour. He seemed to feel our liking for him, and, as the conversation had turned on the inevitable subject of the war, he was making us laugh with stories about pompous and foolish generals. We finished our partridge in this excellent humour. Charlie asked us to have more. We refused. He pressed us. We refused again.

He went on pressing us. Now I had always been taught that it was vulgar to urge people to eat after one refusal. But it came into my head that Charlie had received a present of game, and that he really wanted us to eat more partridge to make up for the rest of the meal. We were young and healthy, a long walk and sea air had sharpened our appetites, and we were both hungry. We gratefully accepted.

In his most splendid grand manner Charlie ordered his manservant to bring us more partridge. And what do you think the man replied? In a tone of resentful insolence he said:

"You can't get more than three portions from one partridge, sir!"

No doubt it sounds absurd, but that was one of the major shocks of my life. My limbs seemed frozen stiff, and yet I could feel my cheeks getting redder and redder with confusion and pity for Charlie. It was as if all three of us had received an insulting smack in the face for which he as host was responsible. I dared not look at him or Marion. It really was horrible to witness so cruel a humiliation of a fellow creature.

I must say Charlie took it magnificently. He made no remark to the man, not even to check him for his insolence in our presence (which I thought superb good manners), ignored our evident bourgeois confusion, and went on talking in exactly the

THE PARTRIDGE

same amusing and charming way. The plates were removed, and we finished the lunch with a little inferior local fruit. We made desperate efforts to respond, but it was hopeless. The ubiquitous loutishness of the world had smashed for ever the fine crystal of our gaiety and good fellowship. We could no longer see Charlie as a romantic original, but only as a wretched and silly old man failing to keep up a pose. I can't remember a single thing he said after the partridge catastrophe, but I do remember the relief with which we said good-bye and the sense of hypocrisy when we promised to "come again."

Marion and I walked back to Eva's in miserable silence. Suddenly Marion exclaimed:
"Wasn't it awful?"
"Awful," I answered.
"Was it our fault?"
"Certainly not," I said firmly, though my own conviction was not so firm as my tone. "He insisted on it. The fault was his."
"But do you think he didn't *know?*"
Marion's voice was shrill and insistent. I resented her probing what I felt as a wound, and I didn't answer. When we got back to Eva's Marion went indoors to finish packing, and I tramped up and down the garden path for an hour or more before I felt calm enough to go and make polite farewell conversation with Eva.
We never saw Charlie again.

Jolly Girls

Jolly Girls

"OH, BUT she's such a *jolly* girl," said the voice defensively; and there wasn't any need for defence, for I didn't know the girl and had formulated nothing for or against her. But evidently this was the form of apology devised by her "friends." Sometimes when I listen to the "friends" of girls, I wonder what the devil sort of harpies their enemies may be. . . .

". . . such a *jolly* girl." That flat little pebble of a phrase went ricochetting over my mind. It is odd—or perhaps it isn't, but it's a fact—that we have invented no method of recording actual mental processes, nothing but a few improvements on the original hieroglyphs. Certainly that end isn't achieved by the "stream of consciousness" writing, because all the time something in the mind is recording, sifting, rejecting, arranging with extreme rapidity the suggestions, part thought, part image, part feeling, which start up, no doubt from the unconscious. Yet to be comprehensible I must arrange the almost simultaneous responses of a second or two seriatim, impose a false lineal logic, as if one were required to reduce a globe to straight lines. I don't see consciousness as something running on a one-way track, but as a delicate recording centre acted on from many sides in many ways, dilating or contracting to accept or reject.

The voice spoke from behind me, so though I can't see out of the back of my head I can evidently hear that way. An immediate feeling was one of dislike for the word "jolly." I refused instinctively to accept it. It is one of the pretence words, not a mere lazy-mind word like the common man's "bloody"— which simply means "very"—but a nasty middle-class *suggestio falsi* word to which I am expected to respond with an appropriate false reaction of sympathy. I refuse to respond. I feel my face muscles tighten a little in opposition; no doubt I've already begun frowning, refusing to play that particular game. I *won't* accept the "jolly" girl on the pretence scheme of "jollity." I'm going to judge for myself. I'm going to see her, not her social badge.

At the same time, or so near as to be indistinguishable, there spring up several half pictures, half feelings about the word "jolly." In a flicker I see and hear the London intellectual affectedly talking about "that awfully *jolly* thing of Mozart's." It is in fact a poignant adagio. It isn't, never was, never could be "jolly." Only, the man was too impure, too would-be original to say "moving" or "beautiful." They have even sullied the word retrospectively. Flicker, flicker—and I see Shakespeare's "This life is most jolly," Milton's "Jest, and youthful jollity," both exactly right and true but somehow retrospectively falsified by later misuse, like Coriolanus's "Rats!" Flicker again— I hear the schoolboy "jolly," and loathe again all that school pretence.

But this mind-play is subsidiary, barely conscious. I only recover it by a strong effort of memory. Chiefly I was thinking about the girl who was coming, for she had not yet arrived, though the owner of the voice behind me had seen her and announced her coming. Now I begin to feel the pathos of that "jolly." I've seen these jolly girls and their jollity before. It's pretty well a last ditch in the feminine battle, much more commonplace and desperate than the female highbrow—they haven't even that amount of brains. . . . She will be *una dis-*

JOLLY GIRLS

graziata. A wrong use of the word—originally it meant one in disgrace, then by a peculiarly Italian extension of meaning one who has met with an accident, disgraced born unhandsomely. *Poverina*, poor little one, would be better and kinder. . . .

My five seconds of mental flickering are over. She arrives. She isn't a bit of a *poverina*, not the very least—a whacking great lump of a woman in a bathing dress, with red arms and lumpy legs and a lumpy sort of face in spectacles. Aggressive. Already she is laughing like the traditional horse. So that's her line—aggressive, not responsive jollity. She doesn't make me feel a bit jolly.

Introductions. Intentionally she doesn't "get" my name at first, though she knows it perfectly well—a stale old trick, but never mind. I don't rise to attention at the wonder of womanhood in the orthodox way. The reason is that my knee has been broken, is still in a steel and leather splint, and that to rise and sit down is a laborious and rather painful process. She knows this perfectly well too, has seen me cautiously limping about, but nevertheless chooses to be offended. However jolly a girl is she knows a man who doesn't pay ordinary decent homage to women by getting up must be a cad. I wonder a little at the obtuseness of women—don't they know that these ready spring-to-attention men are often the very ones who've been saying and thinking foul things about women half a minute earlier? There are better ways of honouring women, but never mind.

It would be a lie to say the encounter was a social success, but I at least found it interesting—this eternal mystery of other people's lives, the apparently insoluble problem, not of how they live (which is only too obvious) but why. The jolly girl refused a chair, perhaps a glance at my caddishness in not standing up, evidently a hint that she wasn't going to hobnob with *us*. So she stood formidably against the sky, and we could examine her inelegant proportions at leisure. A peasant woman gone pudgy, I thought; a peasant without the spareness of hard diet, the elasticity of strong muscles, the fine upright swinging carriage which comes to those who carry burdens on their heads. Wouldn't the jolly girl be happier and healthier hoeing turnips than pretending to be a lady? She accepted a drink, and sipped it standing, full of righteous disapproval of us, a sort of British Israelite passing over from nothing to nowhere.

What did we talk about? Here my memories are very vague. Stupidity is strangely infectious. When I am with stupid people my intelligence abruptly switches off and retires into some mental background, whence it sardonically observes—observing among other things that I am talking with contemptible vapidity. "Who hath given man speech and who hath set therein" such opportunities for saying the obvious and the imbecile? Unwilling to be cumbered by the stupid phrases spoken and listened to, my memory has totally rejected them. I seem to remember hazily the jolly girl talking about some jolly people—awful mutts—and about tennis. She must have talked about tennis. But what did she add to our knowledge of that superb exercise? Only, I think, that it is jolly. We murmured acquiescence with a social hypocrisy which at this distance astounds me. Why didn't we say what we think, that the cult of tennis is a bore? Her tennis was only part of the jolly pose, a thing that is done.

We switched on to the bathing—that, of course, was jolly too. No doubt about it, it was jolly good. Somebody—it wasn't I—remarked how pleasant it was to come from a wintry England to a climate where one could bathe all day. This seemed to sting the jolly girl, who at once announced loudly and unnecessarily that she was patriotic. In fact, she went on boasting about her patriotism until she finished her drink and went away. Of course she was "patriotic"—a war would give her something to do, feed her self-importance. I wondered how often she had delivered this discourse on her patriotism—she evidently had it

JOLLY GIRLS

by heart. Patriotism, my country right or wrong, white feathers for slackers, binding up the wounds of heroes, a romance with an unsophisticated and lonely subaltern, tableau. You could put it to music, beginning with Rule, Britannia! and ending with the wedding march. It was, I reflected, the jolly girl's only chance of getting a kick out of life, or rather, a kick into death. Let's have another war, and all be jolly together. And if there isn't another war, well, I could imagine how well the "patriotism" would go down with the penny-newspaper men she knew. With that face and advancing embonpoint, it was no good her attempting the fanfrolic sex stuff of the suburbs. No good at all. But being jolly and patriotic—something told me she must also be "unselfish to the marrow"—might land a curate.

Somehow I didn't see the jolly girl as a perpetual spinster. She hadn't given up all hope, I could swear. Doubtless, that clean straight hero from the illustrated magazine would never turn up; but nowadays there are so many poor and lonely youngish men and they all invariably marry. Someone, some lonely bachelor, would swear before God to endow her with two-fifty a year and Aunt Sylvia's furniture, and she would swear to honour and obey him. She'd make a jolly good wife, and jolly well make her husband toe the line too. And a jolly good mother—no scrimshanking out of the O.T.C. for *her* sons. I could see their names living for ever—on a granite slab read by nobody. . . .

It is written, Blessed are the poor in spirit. If it means, to blazes with the pseudo-intellectuals, then I agree. But if it means, Blessed are the fatheads, I can't agree. Give me the rich, the abounding in spirit. There aren't so many of them. Possibly the jolly girls are to be numbered among the poor in spirit, but I certainly find their spirit oppresses mine. They give me that feeling of uneasiness and shame which you experience at a thoroughly bad play or at seeing a man making a public fool of himself. How can they be content to pick up the shabbiest silliest shallowest newspaper ideas and activities, and think they are living? Poor in spirit indeed! Such poverty is frightening. We talk pompously of abolishing the slums, never of abolishing the slum mind. But slums are the result of the slum mind—in Italy you may see palaces which have been turned into slums. And even in the slums there is a crude swarming sort of vitality. There is a washed poverty of living which is almost worse; it is so devitalized, so bored, so false that its only hope is a war in which to immolate itself in unconsciously wished-for death. Meanwhile—play at being jolly. What a lugubrious farce! I shiver.

Letter to a Young Man

Letter to a Young Man

DEAR JOHN,—I have just realized that in a few days you'll be twenty-one. Congratulations. I enclose a small offering in that form which experience has showed me is most grateful to the young, *i.e.*, ready cash. No obligations are attached, spend it as you want yourself.

At the same time I am sending this rather boring letter. I shouldn't wonder if you drop it in the waste-paper basket without reading it. Such is the natural fate of those who interfere.

The year of your birth—1914—is one that has unforgettable associations for people of my age. Suppose you had been born in 1898, sixteen years earlier—a longish time, I admit, but not so very long. Well, if you had been, twenty-one years later you'd have been in the Army for at least a year or wounded or dead. You couldn't have escaped it. At the present moment you haven't the slightest desire to be in the Army or wounded or dead. I'm quite sure you look forward to doing a lot of other things in the future and that you have your own plans for getting the best out of life. And quite right too.

Only—in the year you were born there were millions of young men in Europe making plans for their lives, as you are; and within four and a half years millions of them were dead. So far as you are concerned the tragedy of those deaths and of all

ARTIFEX: SKETCHES AND IDEAS

the accompanying suffering might be as remote as Waterloo and Troy. They haunt and will always haunt the memory of those of my age, but it is right that you should not be concerned about them. But your life now and in the future will be influenced by the results of that war. And there is always the possibility, indeed probability, that sooner or later you will be faced by a situation of the same kind.

What would you do if it arrived?

Don't say: Time enough to think about that when it does come. Believe me, that only means that you will be bewildered and drift into what seems easiest. Far better think it out now in calmness, and have your decision ready. Besides, you will have some sort of influence in the world. If you refuse to face this issue, you are merely joining the mob of drifters; if you do face it, you can at least contribute your share to averting an occurrence which, I assure you, is no joke, especially for men of military age. We came very close to the edge of complete collapse last time. It seems fairly certain that in another large-scale contest everybody will be involved, and what if anything will survive is a query. So the question is far from being an academic one. On your answer and the answer of the millions of men of fighting age throughout the world the fate of humanity depends.

Of course, in a sense the question is an unfair one. You didn't make the world, you cannot influence the governments and the armament makers, you are not responsible. Quite true. But then, are you absolutely willing to resign your fate into other people's hands, without the slightest effort to assert your own convictions? In this vast mass movement the influence of one person seems and indeed is trivial; but then masses are eventually made up of units. At the moment, only a small minority has the active will to war; another, possibly larger, but less powerful minority has the active will to peace. In between is a huge number of passive peace-hopers who could fairly easily

LETTER TO A YOUNG MAN

be turned into war-willers, and possibly an equally large number who refuse to bother about it. Still, one active peace- or war-willer can and does influence others. And as you would be among the first to pay the price if a great war did occur, it seems only common sense for you to find out what you really think about it, what your answer would be to my question.

I don't know what your answer would be. You might, for instance, say that you rather look forward to a war—opportunities of great and stirring actions and emotions. Alas, your actions would remain obscure, and at least 90 per cent. of your emotions would be boredom and dread. You mightn't even have much time for those. But do you really look forward to the prospect of killing other people or—which is more probable—being eventually killed by them, in obedience to a set of newspaper catchwords masking purposes which are not defined and aims which are not realizable? War is a criminal lunatic's method of solving difficulties and disputes. All it decides is which side is the stronger; victory is no guarantee of superior wisdom. The victor can indeed "dictate terms," but for every problem he settles he creates a crop of new ones. The present state of Europe is more confused, uneasy and unhappy than it was in 1914. The gigantic effort of 1914–1918 having resulted in confusion worse confounded, how can one expect anything but the same result from another war? Any ameliorations which have occurred have been in spite of the war. And the result of "vanquishing" the Germans and "dictating terms" is that they would just as soon fight as go on as they are! There is the wisdom of war. We fight to end German militarism, and find after nearly twenty years that we have made it more militant than ever.

But I am sure you are familiar with the arguments against modern war, which in England at any rate have been widely disseminated. And of course the strictest military frontier cannot keep people inside it from thinking. It may be that the military pomp and boasting which come from Italy and Germany are a measure of the resistance the war-willer must now try to overcome. The danger with us is that we should take these peace arguments for granted, or overdo them. It is a mistake to be unjust to the soldier and his ideals.

I've said that in war you'd find 90 per cent. of your emotions were boredom and dread. This may or may not be true; but if if it is so, think of the virtues necessary to endure them over a long period of time. The modern soldier is not a robber or a degraded brute or even a fool. He may be misguided, and after the stress of fighting may and does fall into excesses which the same man would not commit in ordinary circumstances. But an extraordinary, an abnormal excitement accompanies a battle. What happens to the various glands I don't know, but I do know that the pulse is greatly increased for a period of from fourteen to twenty hours after action—I have tested this with a battalion doctor. So, in spite of the excesses, I still say that the soldier must and does exhibit some of the so-called human virtues. Abnegation, self-control, acceptance of hardship and pain, self-sacrifice, subordination to a purpose believed to warrant sacrifice, devotion to friends, even sometimes pity to enemies. I sometimes think that war is so willingly accepted because it asks so much of men; and that peace is despised because it seems to ask so little. The "virtues" of men destroy them.

This appeal I think the most insidious of all, the most difficult to resist. To ardent spirits it is almost irresistible when a leader says: "I offer you hunger, hardship, terrible tests of endurance, wounds and death, for the sake of our cause." While there is generosity in men that trumpet call will outblast meek piping for a safe job and a nice little home. It is a fearful splendour in war that it gives the common man the chance to discover with amazement the greatness and the beauty of moral force that are in him.

Now, if, as I hope, you are willing to be on the active side for peace, you must find an answer to this appeal. You must ask: For what cause? The answer may be various, but it is certain to include: For your country. I snatch the words from a German nationalist poet and say: Dein Vaterland muss grosser sein, your country must be greater. In our world today these combats of nations are as petty as the squabbles of feudal lords. The only cause worth fighting for is a world cause. The only force in which you can enlist is a world force. If they won't give you that cause, don't fight. You will be wasting your virtues. What do England and Germany matter, what is Italy? Love your country, if you will, but love the world more. It is a beautiful world.

But there is no world force, no world authority to wield it. Ask for it, go on asking for it. Dein Vaterland muss grosser sein. Do not defend England. It is a great nation, but it must submit to something greater, as Provence submitted to France and Tuscany to Italy. A dream? What a dream was modern France in the fifteenth century! Perhaps the greatest nations will have to give up most for this dream. To whom much is given ... The alternative is strife, collapse, despair. You will need most of the virtues of the soldier if you strive sincerely for peace. And even if you succeed, you won't have a perfect world. Far from it. For one thing, you will have created a state of things, from which there will be escape for a dissentient minority. But this experiment of world government and world peace must be tried. Perhaps it will fail, and men will break away into separateness again. Perhaps it will succeed and men will discover what they mean by "living." I myself have no love for a suburbanized world, but I believe that we must go on, and not turn back, dismayed by the prospect of a universal Switzerland. I dislike Switzerland very much, but there is really no reason why the world should not be more intelligent and interesting than the Swiss.

I don't suggest, you see, the usual conscientious objection to

ARTIFEX: SKETCHES AND IDEAS

shedding blood. To establish order there must be the force to compel it. And that means bloodshed. Still less do I denounce national war, and cry up the class war, the bloodiest of all. But I do see a world force, moving swiftly and ruthlessly against any of these petty egotistic national groups—England or Germany or the United States—which might dare to break the world peace.

Incidentally, it would be a devilish tough job. But I hope you would refuse anything less.

I must warn you that there are many forces and arguments, some cogent, against this programme. There might, for instance, be a ghastly and mediocre sameness over the whole world. But, under a world power, people might and would be free to develop all their local individualities without quarrelling over them. They might, but then they might not. But, as it is, a mediocre uniformity is spreading over the world, and men are being highly truculent about differences which are not even distinctions. Only, do remember that all the "reasons" alleged for war between nations are false ones. Their alleged objects are more likely to be obtained by peaceful and reasonable methods. The root motive of war-willers finally resolves itself into the desire to show themselves superior to others by killing or triumphing over them. And that is not superiority of a kind which the world now accepts. Do we believe that the Japanese are "superior" to the Chinese because of the affair in Manchukuo? On the contrary, the whole world knows that the Chinese are the greater civilization. Which is not to assert that the lesser may not destroy the greater. The clumsy bully can always destroy. The question to ask is: What can he create?

A last question before I end this enormously long letter. Granted the achievement of a stable world peace, what then? Are we still to go on with this petty getting and spending, this dreary ideal of economists and scientists? I think you will admit

LETTER TO A YOUNG MAN

that while scientists may know a great deal and provide vast power, they have not invented a great conception of life. That is a point to which we might give our attention—the establishment of life values.

And so, a happy birthday to you.

Female Thinking Extravert

Female Thinking Extravert

IT'S amusing how one thing leads to another. I was reading one of these absurd modern books of "psychology"—the kind of book which quite seriously talks about "compensatory unconscious functions"—and I came across a sentence which suddenly reminded me of Anita. Being reminded of Anita made me laugh, and that made me put the book down to consider the case of Anita.

You might almost say Anita's family is upper class. At least there is plenty of money and none of them does any work of a profitable nature. Also they're frightfully respectable, so respectable that Anita is one of a family of seven girls. The man who was going to St. Yves in my opinion had a light responsibility compared with Anita's papa, but it didn't seem to worry him. He took the view, common enough at one time but now getting a little fly-blown, that "God had sent" his daughters, all seven of them; so it was up to God to see they were sent to the right place in life. Perhaps that explains why none of them got married.

Although Anita is a joke, she's the brightest of the family—which admittedly isn't saying much. The rest of them are poops, dummkopfs, old-fashioned dolls stuffed with Treasury notes instead of sawdust. Not that they were allowed much

ARTIFEX: SKETCHES AND IDEAS

money, but each of them got an allowance of £250 a year on her twenty-first birthday, with everything found so long as she was at home. Anita was the only one who didn't stay put. She wanted to see life.

Need I say that to justify herself Anita had to be an "artist" and spoil canvas? I think it's about time young women thought out some other alibi, and ceased discrediting the arts. However, that's a piece of sheer professional spite, due to the fact that I'm always having to deal with Anitas who've chosen writing as their particular alibi. And it's a bore.

The old boy was really very decent about it when Anita, all trembling-bold, announced that she intended to live away from home and be Mary Cassatt all over again. He looked at her obliquely and said O.K., but she wouldn't get any more money. And Anita said that was O.K., she didn't expect it. And the old boy said he'd heard a lot about this sort of thing from the Press, and what the dickens they thought they wanted to do he couldn't imagine.

And, really, when you look at Anita it is rather hard to imagine. As soon as she got away she cut her hair very short, and looked like an aged and anxious schoolboy. She had Japanese hair, straight, black and scanty, and her face is the kind which will one day shrivel up like the outside of a walnut. She exhibits far too much silk stocking and not nearly enough chest. Even now, when she's aggressively emancipated, your first reaction on seeing her would be the thought: "Here's a born old maid!" As for her painting, even Anita knew it was gammon from the start.

I've nothing against old maids *per se*, absolutely nothing. They may be perfect pets for all I know, but that kind doesn't seem to come my way. Still, I can't help thinking La Rochefoucauld's epigram applies even better to them than to marriages—they may be good but never delicious. At any rate I'm prepared to swear Anita wasn't delicious; and she never will be.

FEMALE THINKING EXTRAVERT

Just before she left home Anita came to have tea with me. She smoked lots of cigarettes and sprawled in one of my armchairs and talked about things she thought were highbrow. I wouldn't say Anita was Bloomsbury. But she certainly was Bloomsbury purlieus—St. Pancras or High Holborn. It made me uneasy. Presently she said:

"D'you know how old I am?"

I thought she looked about thirty, so to be on the safe side I said:

"Twenty-three?"

"Twenty-five, my dear, though I know I don't look it. And I'm *still* a virgin!"

She announced that not very interesting fact in tones of sombre gaiety, as if bravely facing a cancer or necrosis of the jaw or something horrible. I didn't know what to reply, so I made comforting noises, strictly non-committal.

"What do you think I ought to do about it?"

I didn't know. All I knew was that *I* wasn't going to do anything about it, so I said firmly:

"I see no reason whatever why a perfectly nice man shouldn't fall in love with you sooner or later. He might turn up at any moment," I added, hoping against hope.

At once I saw by Anita's face that I'd said the wrong thing. Gradually it came out. Bloomsbury purlieus don't believe in "falling in love," won't have it at any price, won't touch love with the end of a barge pole. No doubt I looked puzzled, for she condescendingly explained that "one" had to have sexual experience of the right kind or "one" developed complexes and couldn't admire the best modern poetry or be eligible for the communist party. So all I could do was to wish her the best of luck, as we used to do with trench raiding parties. I wondered how soon she'd get a blighty.

Now, in my opinion, few human spectacles are so charming as two young people downright crazily in love with each other.

ARTIFEX: SKETCHES AND IDEAS

For such I'm always willing to put a rose-crown on my bald head and to shout "Hymen, Io Hymen" or words to that effect, and blow the Registrar. But Bloomsbury purlieus, "definitely" making up its mind that "one" must be sexy, make me shiver. "Their feelings," said the psychology book, "are slight, and rather than being spontaneous, they arise merely because the situation seems—that is, is thought—to justify such an expression of emotion."

That is Anita to a T. She wasn't in love with anyone. She wasn't in love with love. She wasn't a wanton. She hadn't any particular desires. Men didn't like her, and she didn't really like men. My own belief is that Anita is ahead of her time—she's really one of those neuter workers who are going to be produced by the perfectly organized World State. Hitherto, of course, they've been called "old maids," but that was our ignorance.

At any rate I'm quite convinced that Anita's body didn't want sexual experience, but Bloomsbury purlieus had put it into her not too well-furnished head that she ought to want it. And want it she did with a cold implacability of will which reminded me of the worst excesses of the Niebelungs. I don't know what the devil she thought she was—something dramatic and interesting no doubt—but I do know that she had a bad attack of sex on the brain as less enlightened people get a cold in the head.

During the time when she was first in London she used to lunch frequently at a small restaurant I also used because it was handy for my work. Sometimes she came with men, once or twice with other girls, more often alone. From time to time she sat down for coffee at my table, and related in a hoarse whisper her manifold disappointments. Work as she would, the beastly young men simply didn't come up to scratch. Did I think it was because they wouldn't or because they couldn't?

One day she gave me a start by telling me that she had gone

out the evening before determined to pick up the first man who spoke to her.

"And did you?" I asked.

"No," she said, "I didn't like the look of those who spoke to me, so I walked about, and eventually went home. But I may have to do it sooner or later. . . ."

"Now, look here, Anita," I said crossly. "You're going to give me your word here and now that you'll never do such a thing again, or . . ."

"Or what?"

"Or I'll be a sneak-thief and tell your father. You're not fit to be out of the nursery."

Well, she was very angry with me, and very Bloomsbury purlieus contemptuous, but I stuck to my point and she saw I meant what I said. She knew jolly well that she would lose her £250 a year in no time. One thing I must say in favour of Anita and her purlieus lot—they do know which side their bread's buttered. She would have hated to lose that money. Anyway, eventually she gave me her promise, and I accepted it. But I was annoyed with her; and I felt that as a very left left-winger it was tactless of her to try to gate-crash into an old-established union as a black-leg of the most frivolous sort. . . .

For some time after that I only exchanged nods or waves with Anita as we passed each other in the restaurant. Then one day, looking up from my prunes and rice, I saw Anita bearing down on me ruthlessly.

"Hullo," I said uncordially.

"Hullo. May I sit at your table?"

"Of course—I've got to go in a moment."

Anita sat down. Rather quickly the sensation crept over me that Anita had something a little queer about her. I hardly knew how to describe it, rather like an overcharged electric battery which has simply got to shock somebody. Evidently she wanted badly to tell me something. So I wearily and weakly caved in to the great female will, and asked:

ARTIFEX: SKETCHES AND IDEAS

"How are you getting on? What have you been doing lately?"

"The *most* lovely time," said Anita, smiling in a coy manner I found inexpressibly unpleasant.

"Oh? I'm glad of that. . . ."

"Last night," Anita interrupted, "I went to a divahn place—we all dance naked, you know."

"I didn't know. Isn't it rather cold and don't you stub your toes?"

She gave me the sort of look which used to be called "withering," but I didn't wither. I half-guessed what was coming.

"And," she added importantly, almost smugly, "I spent the night with Rudolf."

"Rudy Marston?"

"Yes."

I don't know what Anita expected from me, because I don't know what is the right thing to say in such circumstances in the purlieus. As a fact, I said nothing. I was thinking. So at last Anita had realized—no, that's the wrong word—had *fulfilled* herself. I wondered what she now felt full of. And poor Rudy, I thought, just down from Cambridge and can't yet carry his liquor like a gentleman. . . .

All this time Anita watched me, eagerly waiting for what I should say, no doubt in order to give me the complete bulletin. As I said nothing the look of expectation faded from her face. Evidently she thought I was such a hayseed that I hadn't understood. She cleared her throat.

"Sexual intercourse," she announced proudly, "took place—twice."

I laughed. I laughed loud in the way you mustn't laugh among intellectuals. I went on laughing.

Anita hasn't spoken to me since. And when my name's mentioned in front of her I'm told she elevates her fulfilled nose and remarks: "*That* fool!"

And upon my word I'd just as soon have it that way.

Ethics of Authorship
"Sweet are the uses of advertisement."

Ethics of Authorship
"Sweet are the uses of advertisement."

IS THERE a book racket? Of course there is. People talk of it openly; some deplore it, some accept it, some profit by it; nobody does anything much about it.

By "book racket" I mean efforts to sell literary wares by hook or by crook, chiefly crook. Authorship ideally is partly a trade but chiefly a profession, but the latter status has been wholly forfeited by practices which would be considered indecent and intolerable in "mere" doctors, solicitors and barristers. Authorship now is self-convicted as a trade, using all the methods considered appropriate in "pushing" cigarettes, soap, petrol and women's clothes, with the addition of practices which might be considered illegitimate in ordinary commerce.

Among authors it is customary—if they are eccentric enough to object to this state of affairs—to place the whole blame upon the greed and low moral standards of publishers and booksellers. According to them, *authors* don't drive hard bargains or pine for large incomes, authors don't want splash advertising, controlled (and hence favourable) reviews, social and news paragraphs, interviews, booksellers' displays, books of the month. Authors don't want to deliver addresses at places where books are sold and afterwards autograph copies of their works for purchasers. Authors don't want their photographs in the

ARTIFEX: SKETCHES AND IDEAS

Press nor do they want to sign them for admirers. Authors "cannot be bored" with answering fan letters or supplying autographs for the unique collection which is being made for the twenty-first birthday of that blue-eyed little girl in the Middle West. Their sensitive feelings as artists are lacerated at the thought of their works appearing in "cheap periodicals" which pay well and invariably have a flapper's head in colours on the cover; and they shrink from the polluted dollars which are the price of shame for allowing feeble travesties of their masterpieces to appear on the movie screens of the world before the coarse gaze of multitudes. . . .

Speaking as an author, I say that if we are going to talk about the book racket let's begin by criticizing ourselves. How many of the above-noted practices would go on if authors didn't demand them? If you are an author, you can test this. Go to your publisher when your next book is being printed and say: "I am certified as sane, and I hereby declare that I do not desire splash advertising or that any steps should be taken to influence reviews or to secure pars. I don't want my photograph in the papers or in booksellers' windows. Let your blurb be modest and your jacket unassuming." At first, of course, the publisher will be suspicious. He will say: "Come, come, Mr. Shakespeare, a truce to this pleasantry" or something like that. But if you can convince him of your sincerity (a difficult feat, I admit) he will certainly shows signs of deep emotion. Probably he will clasp you in his arms and shed tears. He will certainly take you to his Club after having boasted about you to his friends, and other publishers will saunter past to take a respectful view of The-Author-Who-Didn't-Want-To-Be-Puffed.

This gratifying experience will have to be paid for, however. Several months later your agent will look glum when you see him, and will have to inform you that owing to the rapid spread of cretinism among the reading public, well . . . in short, this book hasn't done as well as the last one. He thinks (subject to

ETHICS OF AUTHORSHIP

your approval) that he ought to see the publisher and arrange for a properly organized advertising campaign. Meanwhile, he has an offer for you to lecture in U.S. at five hundred dollars a throw. Do you agree? Yes? Well, what about a spot of lunch at the Savoy?

Let me pause a moment and relate a slight historical anecdote which will set the scale by which the progress of the present century may be estimated. Considerably less than a century ago a few modest lines appeared in *The Athenaeum*, announcing that next week Mr. B. (I've forgotten his name) would publish the Poems of Mr. Dante Gabriel Rossetti. There was a frightful row. Rossetti was furious and said it was ignoble puffing of the worst sort, and that the publisher ought to be hanged in chains. I don't know how he was quieted down; probably not with caviar and eighteen-inch cigars.

This Rossetti anecdote—one must make allowances for Victorian prejudices, must one not?—will serve as prologue to a little dialogue of Authors, entitled "The New Deal."

Scene: Smoking Room of a Club. A. is seated, reading a wad of tattered press cuttings. Enter to him B. from whose pockets bulge another wad of press cuttings.

A. Hullo old man, haven't seen you for a devilishly appropriate number of donkey's years.

B. Well, I'm surprised to see you here. I heard you'd retired to Cornwall on a small compassionate allowance from the Literary Fund. *I've* been in America.

A. Lecturing to the hicks? Must be a dismal job. Not worth the candle. They offered me a thousand a Lecture and I refused.

B. Pounds?

A. (Reluctantly) Dollars.

B. Pooh! That's nothing. I've been getting five thousand a week at Hollywood.

ARTIFEX: SKETCHES AND IDEAS

A. Dollars?
B. Pounds.
A. What were you acting—King Kong or Caliban?
B. Nothing of the sort. I was re-writing Shakespeare and Flaubert for the talkies. And, by Jove, my dear chap, you can't imagine how much they're improved by judicious cutting and modernizing.
A. No, I can't. Did you have a good time?
B. Wonderful, absolutely wonderful. Reporters met me on the boat at New York and again when I left. Quintupled the sale of my books. Look here. (Produces cuttings.)
A. Is that all? Look here. (Shows his own.) Full pages most of them, and photos in every one.
B. I didn't know you were doing publicity work for Priestley—shouldn't have thought he needed it.
A. I'm not. These are mine, mine, *mine!*
B. About you?
A. Yes, why not?
B. Good lord!
A. Have a look at them.
B. Oh, I take your word. How did you manage it?
A. That's my secret.
B. Oh, all right. How did the book go?
A. Magnificently, my dear chap, magnificently. A riot. Stuggins and Blobb tell me that for a fortnight they were so busy sending it out they had to engage extra packers and suspend the sale of all other books.
B. How many copies?
A. Up to last Saturday 74,315.
B. Not bad. I did 91,001 in three months with my last.
A. Which was that? "Bad Odours?"
B. No, that was the last but one. "Drink To Me Only."
A. I didn't know it was out. But, I say, do your figures include Colonial sales?

ETHICS OF AUTHORSHIP

B. Yes, of course.

A. Oh, that puts a different face on it. In addition to my 74,315 English I had 18,347 Colonials—which puts me ahead.

B. What do you get on Colonials?

A. 20 per cent. on published price.

B. So do I. That's the usual, isn't it?

A. I believe so, and 35 per cent. on English. At least, that's what I get.

B. 35? Oh, I get 40.

A. 40! My dear sir, that's impossible. With booksellers $33\frac{1}{3}$, that leaves only $26\frac{2}{3}$ for the publishers. They'd lose on every copy.

B. Not in my case. The booksellers only get a discount of 15 per cent. from me, and jolly glad to take it, what with all these unsaleable books.

A. Well, I say it's impossible, and I can't believe it.

B. Well, come to that I don't believe you either.

A. What d'you mean? Are you insinuating that I overstate my figures? Look at last week's "Sunday Multiplier."

B. I did, but I didn't see anything about you in it.

A. Good heavens! There was a full-page ad. Didn't you see Laurel Bellowes said "Drink to Me Only" was the greatest novel that ever had been or ever would be written?

B. I shouldn't believe anything Laurel said.

A. And yet you expect me to believe your 40 per cent.

B. That's much more credible than your 91,000.

A. Mine was chosen as the book of the month by Stymie, the great golfers' paper, which has a circulation of nearly a million.

B. And mine was book of the month of the Boilerworkers' Union.

A. Oh, get out. You make me tired.

B. Sorry to overtax your puny brain.

(*Exeunt severally in what is known as high dudgeon.*)

ARTIFEX: SKETCHES AND IDEAS

This is of course exaggerated for purposes of farce, but it represents accurately enough the attitude of some Hector and Achilles of the best-seller class when they meet. Greater accuracy might have been attained by making them women, but obviously ten thousand swords would have leaped from their scabbards, and I couldn't face that.

Splash advertising of books is objectionable. In itself it is vulgar, and a concession to precisely those gross commercial elements of the population which authors should consider it their duty to oppose. Who is going to believe in the integrity and idealism of authors when they employ—or allow others to employ on their behalf—all the most blatant methods of boosting and bally-hoo? If he is careful an author may live from his work without loss of dignity and prestige; but he cannot expect to possess authority or public respect if he descends to the methods of clowns and grocers. If authors continue to measure success in terms of réclame (and what réclame!) and sales then they doom themselves to contempt and impotence.

When questioned, publishers give various excuses for their deplorable incursion into competition with the fag and bottle trades as advertisers. I may interject here that two professional advertising agents I have consulted could hardly find words to express their contempt for the waste and feebleness of publishers' advertising; but this might be biassed, since it isn't done through agents. One excuse brought forward is that people make up their library lists from the advertisement columns. The answer to that is another question:

"To achieve that purpose is it necessary to print authors' names in letters two inches high, accompanied with fulsome commendations which are both sickening and incredible?"

The answer to that is interesting. The publisher will say that if he advertises less he is afraid that his authors will go to another publisher who advertises more. Deadlock. If this is true—

ETHICS OF AUTHORSHIP

and it may be merely the usual publisher's habit of blaming authors—then the heaviest onus lies on authors.

Another thing publishers hint at rather than say is that if they abolished advertising in periodicals, or even cut it down within the bounds of modesty, they fear their books would receive less attention in the review columns. This is a serious charge, fringing libel, so one cannot particularize. If there are abuses in this direction, I am quite sure they are not general. In the first place, newspapers and newspaper men hate publicity-seekers and dislike giving indirect publicity. In the second place, during many years' work as a reviewer for different periodicals I never received the least hint or pressure to notice the production of one publisher more than another.

Judging from my own experience, I should say that it is entirely a mistake to suppose that favourable notice can be purchased by means of advertising. What is more likely to happen is this. The responsible editor or sub-editor cannot possibly read the books himself, but if he knows (as he must know) that Messrs. X have taken extra space to advertise a certain book, he will naturally assume that they think the book important. Therefore he may tend to select such a book for notice, or to suggest it in cases where the reviewer chooses his own books. I don't see anything corrupt in that, but if it does happen then clearly it would tend to stimulate competitive advertising.

On the other hand, could anybody be found daring enough to assert that reviewing is impartial, impersonal and incorruptible? It may be merely honestly stupid or ignorant, but that is another matter. I think it is also corrupt. A reviewer is often a needy person. He may formulate the observation that the continuation of his job depends on filling the advertising columns, and act accordingly. He may have a financial connection with one or more publishers, and allow that fact to influence his judgment. Publishers may ask him to lunch at the Ritz; well-to-do authors may invite him to meet the peerage at dinner or to do a bit of huntin from their baronial halls; can he be insensible to these *douceurs*, these amiable *pots-de-vin?* A pal in the publicity department of a big publisher gives him a tip about one of our authors; is it always neglected? I say nothing of feuds, jealousies, cliques, and the long arm of coincidence engaged in back-scratching. Could we conceive of a great author who should also be a publisher and editor of a literary paper, we might be inclined to think he would get a good deal of interested praise.

Gentlemen (and ladies) at the Universities, who wisely confine their literary activities to criticizing others, deplore the low standards of contemporary writing. Why don't they do something to raise them? But there can be no doubt that reviewing is both haphazard and prejudiced. God forbid that I should say that reviewers ought to be intelligent; but they might at least be honest. Moreover, if it is decided that their (honest) work is useful then they ought to be decently paid. If a little of the advertising revenue could be diverted to raising the reviewers' wages above dole rates, they might have time to read books. Honest informed reviewing might do something towards raising standards of literary taste, but at present no intelligent person pays the least attention to what reviewers say, and the unspoken judgment of the public is superior to the judgments which appear in print.

A very great number of books is published each year, especially in such popular forms as fiction and biography. Nobody can read or even glance at half of them. There is a reading public which wants new books, but doesn't want to waste its time or its money. It wants to be told how to form its library book list, and it relies on advertising, books-of-the-month, what Mrs. Highbrow said at tea yesterday, what Miss Testube at the Library recommends, and reviews, to tell it what to get. Meanwhile, let us hope, literature continues to trickle unheard

ETHICS OF AUTHORSHIP

and unseen somewhere in the background. Let us hope also that in time authors will come to see that the book racket is contrary to all their best interests, that it degrades them and their trade, that the public have rumbled it, and that advertisement is not equivalent to fame.

What Fools These Mortals Be

What Fools These Mortals Be

I HAVE been doing sums.

The present population of the world is variously estimated, but the average is about 1,900,000,000 people for 1935. The average rate of increase is 1 per cent. per annum.

Now do a little sum in compound interest. You will find that in 1978 the world population will be approximately 2,900,000,000—*i.e.*, an increase of 1,000,000,000 in the next 43 years. In the year 2000 A.D. the population will be 3,600,000,000. A century later it would be astronomical—16,000,000,000.

Here's a pretty kettle of simians.

The statistical average method may be—probably is—illusory. For example, China and India, which account for 750,000,000, have already reached the state predicted by Malthus, *i.e.*, a very small minority of wealthy people, an enormous majority on the minimum subsistence line. Hence the constant menace of famine. These people probably can't continue to multiply, although in fact the populations are increasing at a much more rapid rate than 1 per cent. per annum.

According to the American economists, the optimum population for the world is as low as 350,000,000—that is enough to secure the working of the world machine and yet secure a qualitative as well as quantitative life value for them.

ARTIFEX: SKETCHES AND IDEAS

It is generally agreed that if in England you select 100 young men and women of about twenty, in 40 years some will be dead, a few will have invested incomes, and 60 per cent. will be dependent on charity.

Communism won't save the situation—it merely insures a prolongation of the agony by admitting everybody to the minimum subsistence. The biological law is that all living things tend to breed to the margin of subsistence; and increase of favourable circumstances is immediately followed by a rapid increase in numbers, until the natural checks operate. Until man interferes there is a "balance of nature." Agriculture is only about 7000 years old, during which period men multiplied from a few scattered groups into the world of about 1750. The machines have resulted in another huge increase.

Now, human beings have created the "artificial" state of agriculture and industrialism, but they still continue to multiply in accordance with the crude biological urge. But eventually, despite all "economic systems," however ingenious, the biological checks must come into play, certainly within 200 years, probably in the next 50. If men were still living in the "natural" state (*i.e.*, as food-gathering animals), the "natural" unlimited breeding of the Catholics and Nazis, etc., would be perfectly logical and right. But they don't or won't see that both agriculture and industry are "unnatural." Now, if men are permitted artificially to increase their means of subsistence, why should they not "artificially" control their numbers, to avoid the disastrous checks of the biological law?

The crux of the matter is this: Are men to control their own destinies within the framework of reality, or are they to be forbidden by superstitions of religion, nationalism, etc., to do so in certain important respects? Almost all sexual laws and customs are superstitious, *i.e.*, founded on assumptions which are not in accordance with the physiological, psychological and economic facts. Our sexual feelings are real enough somewhere

WHAT FOOLS THESE MORTALS BE

far underneath, but we are compelled into a fake attitude.

Now, improved methods of production and of distribution, (*e.g.*, Socialism, Communism or even Douglas Credit) may stave off the inevitable for a time. But all efforts to ameliorate human conditions are so much waste of time, until this population question is thoroughly examined. There are two ways, and only two ways, out of the impasse. Follow the present superstitions about breeding and the biological checks must operate. They are: War, Disease, Famine. I put them in that order, because what will happen is first a big war or series of wars for "markets" or "honour" or any pretext to avoid admitting the population pressure. An epidemic or epidemics (like, but greater than, the influenza epidemic of 1918) will follow. The destruction of war and the depletion by the epidemic will result in famine far worse than that of 1919. This will be followed by a peace of exhaustion, followed by the same cycle, until humanity relapses into another middle ages, when the breakdown of social organization will leave the way for greater epidemics and famines, when the population will be reduced very considerably. Then the cycle will begin over again. Meanwhile, all the grace and beauty of life will be extinguished.

The other alternative is frankly Utopian, but the only way out. That is a world control of population, with area quotas, and in many cases orders to reduce. The opposition to this will be tremendous, and even great disasters may not overcome it. The disasters will always be attributed to the wrath of God or the wickedness of other people or some such nonsense. Nevertheless, it might be done, if the present feelings about immorality of sex could be transferred to the real immorality of breeding superfluous children for misery and violent death. There would have to be compulsory birth control, and, in cases of evasion, compulsory abortion and infanticide for all women who exceeded their quota. Women might do this voluntarily if they were left free to choose—in fact, the ideal state would be for them to be graded into mothers and non-mothers. Intolerable interference with the liberty of the subject! Well, war, disease and famine are nastier interferences. The great defect of the present "voluntary" system is that it only applies to certain parts of the world, that huge sections of the world have a system of compulsory breeding and that consequently the worst type is breeding. What responsible person would wish to bring children into this chaos?

It will be possible to go on as we are for some time, provided more and more people will accept and endure a lower and lower standard of living. They will *have* to accept it, or fight, and fighting now means collapse. No doubt, "Agrobiology" can produce more and more rice and wheat and margarine and a few things able to keep body and soul together, and the machines can produce masses of shoddy goods. Still, sooner or later, the check must come, as the agricultural countries are filled up. Whatever may be said, the *quality* of human life must deteriorate progressively for the majority. Whatever may be said, there is no getting away from the fact that on January 1st, 1936, there will be approximately 19,000,000 more people in the world than on January 1st, 1935. By 1941, the increase will already be over 100,000,000. All of them asking for a "higher standard of living."

Give us bread!

Why don't you eat radios and pig-iron and ping-pong balls?

There it is. What do I think will happen? There will be rumours of wars, then wars, then epidemics and famines which will destroy the most highly organized nations, and will leave a welter of militarists. This process will begin somewhere between 1945–70. Possibly a little sooner, possibly a little later. There will be a series of the most ghastly dog-fights for subsistence, in which all "culture" will pretty well disappear. Then after several generations a battered remnant will begin to investigate the few tattered relics of our civilization, and may hit on two ideas: Control of population and control of machinery. As it is we are controlled by our own machines—anything will be sacrificed to a machine—and we are caught in the toils of fecundity. Nevertheless, it is not fecundity that men want, but life. Hence the Life Quest. Therefore, you have got to get down to the problem of understanding what you mean by "Life." If life means scratching along on a bare subsistence level, under the oppression of superstitions, with the perpetual threat of war, disease and famine, then I disrespectfully hand "civilization" back my ticket. I am not going to fight another war. And I am not going to endure the miseries of another war as an *embusqué* or an exile. I profess no exaggerated benevolence for humanity, but I am certainly not going to watch the misery of millions for some idiot catchword invented to mask the imbecility of governments and people to deal with a plain and obvious situation. I shall pop off as painlessly as possible, and leave the Friends of Humanity to dispose of my remains.

The present situation is unreal. We are controlled by superstitions about sex, birth, money, militarism, machinery and the like. There is no "innate purposes" in life—men have to invent them. Those put before us are negative and repressive, and based on ridiculous superstitions, or at any rate unprovable assertions. From Science we take what suits our greed and our superstition, and neglect the rest. If a scientist invents a new death-dealing weapon, it is eagerly snatched up. If another scientist warns us of the dangers of overbreeding or attempts to enlighten us on the true nature of sex, he is disregarded; in some countries he would be made guilty of a criminal offence. Yet, in any sane community, the right breeding of human beings would certainly be considered a more important and moral study than the means of maiming and killing them. Such, however, is not our way. "Public morality" is opposed to it, and therefore public morality will be gassed and bombed and diseased and starved along with the rest.

ARTIFEX: SKETCHES AND IDEAS

You are up against "human nature?" Very well then, study human nature, without prejudice and without superstition—it is surely the most important of all studies. As a matter of fact, a good deal has been discovered, particularly in the last thirty years, but very little practical use is made of it. Our laws are rigid with superstition and ignorance. We "punish" people for having something wrong with their ductless glands or because some irreparable psychological injury was done to them by brutal or superstitious treatment in childhood. Study human nature. It is a more valuable study to us than interesting but abstruse formulae about Space-Time and the structure of the atom. Let us have them by all means, but let us also know what more immediately concerns us. You punish people for issuing books about brothels. Then why do you have brothels, why do you go to them? It is an insanity of superstition.

Nor do I believe that "human nature" is necessarily opposed to a rational regulation of human numbers. You compel women to have children, a painful process; you compel men to go and kill each other. Except that it is more rational and humane, the other process is no more a violation of "human nature." The fact that the laws in many countries compel women to have children, proves that the women don't want them, wouldn't have them if left alone. To provoke an abortion is not the crime that it is to kill a young adult on a battlefield. The people to lock up are the armament-makers, the militarist leaders, the generals and all fighting lunatics. The fact that the laws in many countries compel men to fight, proves that the men might not want to fight if left alone. Then, study human nature, find out why these idiot abuses exist, and act fearlessly.

If you are too lazy and apathetic and superstitious to make the attempt to understand your own minds and bodies, how you are made, how birth can be controlled and babies bred wisely, how many people constitute an optimum population, how the quality of people may be improved, and what is the

WHAT FOOLS THESE MORTALS BE

desirable life—then die! Die, and a good riddance to you. Let the world go back to the better animals, let the forests and wild places come back, and let the morning and evening song of natural life go up from them once more. If the experiment of human civilization fails will it matter very much—except to your compulsorily born children?

The Squire

The Squire

LIKE many other human beings, Charles Waterton of Walton Hall suffered from the world's calumny and misrepresentation. After the publication of his *Wanderings in South America* he was accused of a "strong propensity to dress fact in the garb of fiction." Even though he had ridden regularly to hounds with Lord Darlington, his account of riding a live alligator was received with derision; and his account of the three-toed sloth, afterwards proved to be accurate, met a storm of contempt and contradiction, since it was entirely different from that of Buffon and other authorities who had never been to South America. The Squire met these and other aspersions on his veracity with the candour of a gentleman and the charity of a true man. Time, he said, would prove he was right; and in most cases it did. When he guessed the offender was not malicious but merely an honest blunderer, as like as not the Squire would invite him down to Walton Hall, and gently banter him out of his error, with liberal quotations from the classics. A specimen of the creature in question, preserved with the exquisite skill of which Waterton alone at that time held the secret, would clinch the matter.

Yet there was one calumny which even the great-hearted and good-humoured Squire could not forgive. A closet naturalist, said to be an Oxford man, referred to him in a leisurely aside as "the eccentric Waterton." Whether the Oxford man was right or wrong, perhaps this modest account will show. At any rate the Squire was deeply hurt by that "eccentric," so much hurt that we may be sure the "Oxford man" would never have used it if he had guessed how much his unlucky phrase would haunt the honest old gentleman. Whenever this topic came up, as it frequently did, while he strolled about his park with one of the guests for whom he kept open house, the Squire would pause in his eager talk about the birds and trees and beasts he loved so well, and demand to know if he were eccentric. "But no," he would answer himself; "it is a vulgar calumny. I am the most ordinary, the most commonplace of men. It would be impossible for me to do an eccentric thing, so ordinary am I." And then sitting down to take off his boots, he would add, "But come, my dear friend, let us forget this fellow, *monstrum horrendum, informe*. Mount with me to the top of this noble elm. I want to show you a nest." And up the octogenarian Squire would go, bare-footed on account of his prehensile ("prensile" he called them) toes, as nimbly as a middy up the rigging.

Only England could have bred the Squire and only England could have loved him as he was loved, in spite of that ever regrettable "eccentric." As one of his biographers says:

"It was perhaps eccentric to have a strong religious faith, and act up to it. It was eccentric, as Thackeray said, to "dine on a crust, live as chastely as a hermit, and give his all to the poor." It was eccentric to come into a large estate as a young man and to have lived to extreme old age without having wasted an hour or a shilling. It was eccentric to give bountifully and never allow his name to appear in a subscription list. It was eccentric to be saturated with the love of nature.... It was eccentric to be ever childlike, but never childish."

Charles Waterton, or *the* Squire as he was known to every-

THE SQUIRE

body for twenty miles round Wakefield, was born in 1782 of a very old and staunch Roman Catholic family. In consequence of their obstinate adherence to their Faith, neither he nor any of his family since the days of good Queen Mary "was considered worthy to serve his country in any genteel or confidential capacity." We may regret this ostracism on general grounds, but who can doubt, when he comes to know the Squire, that genteel employment would infallibly have meant his getting himself gallantly killed at Trafalgar or Badajos? For by instinct the Squire was a fighting man. Once in ci-devant Dutch Guiana he successfully opposed a police party sent to arrest a friend of his, and consequently received a peremptory order to wait upon the Governor General. But let us pass the pen to the Squire:

"On my name being announced, he came into the hall. Whilst looking at me full in the face, he exclaimed, in a voice too severe to last long: 'And so, sir, you have dared to thwart the law, and to put my late proclamation at defiance?' 'General,' said I, 'you have judged rightly; and I throw myself on your well-known generosity. I had eaten the fugitive's bread of hospitality, when fortune smiled upon him; and I could not find in my heart to refuse him help in his hour of need. Pity to the unfortunate prevailed over obedience to your edict; and had General Carmichael himself stood in the shoes of the deserted outlaw, I would have stepped forward in his defence, and have dealt many a sturdy blow around me, before foreign bloodhounds should have fixed their crooked fangs in the British uniform.' 'That's brave,' said he; and then he advanced to me, and shook me by the hand."

Whether the Squire's obstinate recusancy was due to family tradition, a Stonyhurst education or his own lack of eccentricity, cannot be known; but, though his son took Sir Robert Peel's oath and was appointed Justice of the Peace, the Squire never would.

ARTIFEX: SKETCHES AND IDEAS

"In framing that abominable oath," he declares energetically, "I don't believe that Sir Robert cared one fig's end whether the soul of a Catholic went up, after death, to the King of Brightness, or descended to the king of brimstone."

So there the matter rested, and anything genteel or confidential remained out of the question. And so the Squire turned his attention to natural history, the true passion of his life after the Church, softening even his misgivings about the National Debt and his indignation with Henry VIII, "our royal goat." Whether "wandering" in the forests of Guiana, among which he made four voyages, or "sauntering" on the Continent, or in the recesses of Walton Park, natural history was the very stuff of the Squire's life. As a boy he was flogged, often and severely, for bird's-nesting, and suggests that as colours are burned into crockery, so the love of nature was flogged into him. At Stonyhurst, the kindly Fathers took a more lenient view, and gave a colour of legality to his irresistible propensity by appointing him "rat-catcher to the establishment, and also fox-taker, fourmart-killer, and crossbow-charger, at the time when the young rooks are fledged." The Squire always declared that he owed to Father Clifford the fact that he did not die in the unhealthy jungles of Guiana, for his master made him promise never to put his lips to wine or to spirituous liquors. He had fevers and chills galore, but thanks to his temperance always recovered.

Endless are the stories of the Squire's doings and "dodges" in the bird-sanctuary of Walton Park, whose two hundred and ninety odd acres he enclosed with an immense wall, at a cost of over ten thousand pounds. He who would comprehend them in all their variety and ingenuity must soak himself in the Essays, the Autobiography (a golden document) and the memoirs of the Squire's friends. It says much for the Squire's popularity that none of his neighbours protested at his fostering innumerable starlings, rooks, carrion crows, hawks, magpies, jays and

THE SQUIRE

owls, at a time when there was no Wild Birds Protection Act, when preserving game was invested with almost Norman sanctity, and birds were looked upon as pests to be destroyed. No fowling-piece was ever discharged in the Squire's territory, and the gamekeeper really was a keeper, not a destroyer, his job being to see that no wild life was interfered with. True, pheasants' eggs vanished, ducklings and young chickens were carried off in hosts, cherries and strawberries suffered devastation, but "he grudged them not." And many an essay was penned in his unhandy style, laden with quotations from Ovid and Horace, in defence of the Squire's feathered darlings.

Waterton's life was distinguished by a kind of generous frugality; he was generous to others and frugal with himself. It is said that his personal expenses never equalled the wages of one of the labourers on his estate. Through living so much with birds he seems to have acquired some of their habits; at least he went to bed with them at eight and got up with them at three. He had a horror of entering beds which had been slept in by other people. As he said, the last inhabitant might have been some lovely form divine, but was just as likely to have been a horrid alderman, "pimply with turtle and curaçao." How was this problem to be met by a man who delighted in travelling? After much meditation, the appropriate Watertonian solution was found—the Squire would sleep on the floor. It took him a fortnight to learn to do this with comfort, and thereafter he never entered a bed. At Walton Hall he slept on the boards of a small uncarpeted room, wrapped in a blanket, with a piece of wood for a pillow. But he was no savage, and rigidly opposed the hirsute mania of the Romantic epoch. At a time when long locks and flowing beards were considered attractive in the young and venerable in the aged, the Squire was clean-shaved by four every morning, and never allowed more than half an inch to his comely white hair. After prayers in his private chapel at four, the Squire dealt with the reports of his bailiff and read

Latin or Spanish until eight was struck by a clock which was said to have belonged to his ancestor, Sir Thomas More. The rest of the day was spent out of doors.

The pursuit of science is thought to render men sceptical, but this was not so in the Squire's case. Himself an honourable man, incapable of deception, he was inclined to believe what he was told. Thus, as we have just seen, his clock was Sir Thomas More's. An inlaid gun given him in Spain was "the identical gun used by the Duke of Alva in the Low Countries," while an ivory crucifix acquired at the same time had been "stolen from a church in Rome by a French General." The Squire made a special journey to Naples to witness the miraculous liquefaction of the blood of San Gennaro, which to his immense gratification duly occurred. Indeed, his candour was such that he was apt to miss the point of eighteenth-century irony, and quotes with triumph a remark made by Sir William Hamilton to the effect that an eruption of Vesuvius ceased directly the relics of San Gennaro came in sight of the mountain.

Perhaps it is unjust to accuse the Squire of being scientific. He was a lover of wild things, especially birds, much as other men love books or music or pictures. Even in Rome he cared much more about birds than for antiquities. Every morning he was in the bird market, looking for rare birds on the stalls, and gently remonstrating with the Romans for eating larks and nightingales. He was greatly interested by noticing that a solitary thrush (the passer solitarius of the Psalmist) had made its nest under the roof of the College of the Propaganda, and only refrained from climbing up to have a look at it, for fear of giving scandal. Scientific names and the new-fangled theories put forward by a fellow named Darwin he could not abide. All living things had been created to the greater glory of God. And as for names, well a Salempenta is a Salempenta, why burden the poor creature with Teius Teguexin? Somebody in America

THE SQUIRE

discovered a hawk and called it Falco Harlani. "Pray," cried Waterton sarcastically, "who or what is Harlani? A man, a mountain, or a mud-flat?"

Now that classification has long been more or less settled, many of us may be more disposed to agree with the Squire than with his opponents, when he says that the true object of zoology is not "to ticket animals in a formal inventory" but "to study their life-nature." It is obvious that the basis of the Squire's activities was not "scientific interest" but delight. Many are the stories of his astonishing success in getting wild birds to breed in the nooks he prepared for them, of his skill in making holly hedges grow more swiftly than any one else could do, and of his saving the lives of trees apparently doomed to decay. Most of the trees in his park were given names, and there were few the Squire had not climbed. On fine days he would climb "to the top of a favourite tree" with Horace in his pocket, and in between the odes keep a sharp eye on the Canada geese and the doings of the gamekeeper. A guest one day found the keeper in grave perturbation. Someone, probably a poacher, had wounded a tree with pellets. "Depend upon it," said the man, "Squire will find it out and I shall have to answer for it." Within four hours Waterton had noticed the wound, and the keeper had to pass a rigid examination.

The Squire's success with all living things he wished to foster was obviously due to the fact that he put himself in their place, so to speak. The first thing was to find out exactly what most suited them, and then to give it them. Some have thought he carried this identification of himself with animals a little far. There is, for instance, the affair of the civetta owls. Who but Waterton would have thought of carrying a dozen owls in "a commodious cage" from Rome to Yorkshire? They scraped through the Genoa customs on the ingenious plea that they were Italianissimi, crossed the St. Gotthard in perfect health, traversed Switzerland and Germany, and came to Aix-la-

Chapelle, where the Squire took a bath. "A long journey, and wet weather," he says, "had tended to soil the plumage of the little owls; and I deemed it necessary, that they, as well as their master, should have the benefit of a warm bath." And bathed they duly were. Unluckily, five of them died of cold that night, and only five of the twelve survived to enjoy the pleasures of Walton Hall.

There can be no doubt, however, that in spite of little accidents like this, the Squire had uncanny power over wild creatures, even the most noisome reptiles, and when occasion offered he was only too glad to display for the pleasure of his friends and the confusion of his enemies. Some of his tales about snakes and alligators in the "Wanderings" had been doubted. Unfortunately, it was not then practicable to import an alligator; otherwise he would undoubtedly have ridden it to hounds with Lord Darlington, as he had ridden one on the banks of the Essequibo. But by a great stroke of luck there one day arrived in Leeds a large box of live rattle-snakes. The Squire invited friends and detractors to a public hall, and before their eyes transferred all the snakes to another box, and then back again, with his bare hands. He modestly explained that he merely took advantage of the reptile's sluggish nature, and offered to teach any one to handle them as freely as he did—an offer unaccountably declined. Who can doubt that this friendliness with rattlers was due to the same kind of sympathy which made him rebuild his stables so that the horses could converse with each other, and arrange his pigsties so that the pigs could bask in the sun, as freely as the Squire himself? He suspended chains across the gates in his paddock, so that the cows could lean comfortably against them without damaging the gates while they passed the time of day with each other. Only thus can we explain his deep interest in that creature so ill-treated by Providence, the Rumpless Fowl.

No account of Waterton can dispense with at least a brief

THE SQUIRE

reference to the Ass Wouralia. In the wilds of Guiana the Squire obtained a supply of the Wourali or Urari poison, used by the natives for their poisoned blow-gun arrows. Waterton was greatly taken with this poison, and much interested in finding an antidote. He tried many, such as immersing the victim up to its neck in water, but apparently never tried the simpler remedy of putting salt in its mouth. That was too simple. He excogitated a truly Watertonian remedy, which singularly enough was successful. A young ass was purchased, stabbed with poisoned arrows in the presence of the Duke of Northumberland, and duly lay down and died. Then, under the Squire's directions, a slit was made in the animal's throat, bellows were applied (the method was afterwards much perfected) and after two hours, the ass stood up, shook its ears, and appeared perfectly well. By the Duke's command the ass was tenderly conveyed to Walton Hall, where it lived in peace and plenty, under the name of Wouralia, for three and twenty years. On its death, the Squire wrote a prose elegy, and offered to perform the same operation on any sufferer from hydrophobia, protesting that he would stand his trial at Leeds Assizes as a murderer before he would neglect any opportunity of saving the life of a fellow creature.

If the Squire was a bit rough with the donkey, it cannot be said that he spared himself in the matter of doctoring. To read his account of how he dealt with "a smart attack of fever" may well make the flesh creep on the stoutest. Appallingly large doses of jalap and calomel were assisted by frequent and abundant blood-letting. The Squire believed in the lancet (perhaps it had been favoured at Stonyhurst in his day) and usually operated on himself. In his old age he told a friend that he had blooded himself one hundred and thirty-six times. Since his usual measure was from twelve to twenty ounces, the reader may well pause in awe at the thought of such an effusion of blood. But such things were trifles to the hardy Squire. In

ARTIFEX: SKETCHES AND IDEAS

Guiana, he investigated the habits of the vampire bat and its blood-sucking propensities. He saw quantities of the bat; he saw the wounds it made in cattle and in human toes; and he longed to be able to say that a vampire had sucked his blood. Night after night the Squire slept with his naked toe hopefully sticking out of his hammock. But could he succeed in his wish? No! "The provoking brute refused to give my claret a solitary tap."

The immunity of the Squire's toe to vampires may have been due to hardening of the epidermis by going bare-foot. Considering the nature of the growth in tropical forests, one would think stout boots and puttees the best wear, but the Squire said that one should go bare-footed. And bare-footed he went. Bare-footed he was on the famous occasion when he captured the large live snake which "instantly sprang at my left buttock, seized the Russia sheeting trousers with his teeth, and coiled his tail round my right arm." Bare-footed he entered Rome for the first time. The public talk about this last feat distressed the Squire. It was said that he had done this from reverence to the eternal city. He had no claim to such merit, he protested. He had walked the last fifteen miles, yes; and yes, bare-footed; but it was simply because he had been accustomed to do so in Guiana. Unluckily, the Pope's pavement seems to have been harder than the Guiana swamps. The Squire took the skin off his feet, and was laid up for three weeks.

Ghastly accidents befell this intrepid investigator of Nature, and his death at eighty-three was due to a heavy fall in his own grounds. It is pleasanter to turn from these to his climbing feats, which began at eight and lasted until eighty-two. There he had only one accident, and that was due (at sixty-eight) to his using a queer ladder of his own devising, despite the agonized pleadings of his son. Down he came and broke his arm badly, from which he drew the moral that it was unsafe to use ladders in climbing trees. His most famous feat in climbing re-

THE SQUIRE

sulted in no such disaster, and occurred in 1817, when the Squire (then aged thirty-five) was in Rome.

". . . I fell in with my old friend and school-fellow, Captain Jones. Many a tree we had climbed together in the last century; and, as our nerves were in excellent trim, we mounted to the top of St. Peter's, ascended the cross, and then climbed thirteen feet higher, where we reached the point of the conductor, and left our gloves on it. After this, we visited the castle of St. Angelo, and contrived to get on to the head of the guardian angel, where we stood on one leg."

The Squire omits to add that the Pope ordered the gloves to be removed instantly, since they rendered the lightning conductor useless. Nobody could be found bold enough to attempt the task, so in the unwanted presence of a large and delighted Roman audience, the Squire had to go up again and fetch his own gloves.

And here we may appropriately take leave of the Squire, standing on one leg on the head of an angel. Who that has grown to love him can ever hereafter pass the Castello without thinking of that spare figure poised so perilously over the City, which embodied for him a loyalty superior even to ornithology and the British uniform? His noble park and all its "dodges," if it still exists, must be smoke-blackened and withered by the exhalations from that human hell, the Black Country. If the Squire could return to his old haunts, he would scarcely be able to watch the great flights of rooks going westward to feed, as he loved to do. His science, such as it was, is obsolete; his Wanderings superseded; but the memory of his great heart and noble whimsical nature will live on in the hearts of some of his countrymen.

D. H. Lawrence

D. H. Lawrence

A GREAT deal has been written about the personality of Lawrence—quite rightly, because he was one of the most original and interesting persons of his time. We have to go back to Shelley and to Burns to find writers whose personal characters are as unique and striking as his. But the amount of personal writing about him seems disproportionate when you think how very little competent interpretation has been published about his writings. And yet, though his memory will live on as a great character among English writers, the imperishable part of him lives in his books. I have no hesitation in saying that most comment on Lawrence's books—especially that in newspapers—is worthless rubbish, turned out by people who have either not read him at all or have read him so hastily, stupidly and unfairly as to amount to the same thing. It is an unpleasant feature of our time that when "critics" are given a great new writer they spend their small energy looking for flaws, never in the discovery of beauties and great qualities. The society of Lilliputians do their best to patronize Gulliver. The comment perishes; Lawrence's work remains and will remain.

It would be absurdly pretentious to claim that I can give here any adequate summary of Lawrence's gifts as a writer or of his considerable and varied output. At most I can throw out a few

ARTIFEX: SKETCHES AND IDEAS

hints of what seem to me to be the obvious lines of an intelligent appreciation.

Lawrence is a great literary artist. By this I don't mean that he was a painful planner and polisher—an artist in the sense that Flaubert and Pope were artists. I mean that he was greatly *gifted* as an artist, if only because he possessed a most delicate and most passionate sensibility. His art was an art of spontaneity, fresh quick-flowing creativeness. I won't say he never blotted a line, because he re-wrote some of his novels more than once; but the re-writing was not laborious correction, it was a totally new effort at creation when the earlier effort had failed to satisfy him. His most eloquent and faultless pages came as easily to him as those which seem most careless. Except when he loses his temper, the note is never forced.

Lawrence's sheer natural gifts as a writer of English prose are a wonder. As far back as 1914 I felt the strange power and beauty of his handling of our language when he is at his best. And now when I re-read his complete output I am more than ever filled with wonder and admiration for the abundance and variety of his writing. A superb anthology could be made of Lawrence's prose, from the poetical-prose passages alone. It was Lawrence who brought back poetical vision to the novel, Lawrence who gave back physical reality to English literature, Lawrence who rejected the social relations of men as a theme and concentrated on essential, intimate vital relations. He freed us from the Fabians.

It is not true to say that he was merely a descriptive or impressionist writer. True, he is a very personal writer, a lyric novelist, but very few writers have been so sensitively and profoundly aware of all that was outside themselves. He can enter the very soul of another man or woman, animal, flower or tree, place or landscape, and interpret them with a vividness which makes his experience of them our own. It is not mere knowledge he gives us—there are forty thousand academic writers

D. H. LAWRENCE

bursting with deadly knowledge; Lawrence gives us his vital burning experience.

Why then was he persecuted? What then was his sin? I will tell you. First, he was unswervingly true to the experience and truth of the moment; so that, like Renan, he would unsay today what he said yesterday, and tomorrow deny both. But where Renan was perpetually sceptical, Lawrence perpetually renewed his faith. Yes, if you will, he was inconsistent; as human life and the ceaselessly changing universe are inconsistent. Consistency is the virtue of dull sterile writers—they lack the flame that consumes and renews. And the age of "Safety First" prefers the sterile dullard to the living flame. But crime as that is, it was not his worst crime. He hated pretence, and English society is pretence from top to bottom. It is the ceaseless boring pretence and pretentiousness which make the moral atmosphere of England unbreathable. Lawrence crashed through the sacred pretences as if they were paper hoops; and since there is even more pretence about sex in England—or was until recently—than anything else, he went through that particular paper hoop with a resounding crash. That was his sin—a complete detestation of English pretence. It is useless, I know, to say this to the elderly generations—I say it to the younger who will understand me.

As for the intellectuals—they have never really understood him, and therefore could never really be for him. Inasmuch as he was persecuted by the "bourgeois," they supported him, tried to make a feeble "cause" of him. But how could they truly like one who was so contemptuous of them and their pretentions? It may cause a mild shock to "literary London," but I can say from personal knowledge that Lawrence didn't care a brass farthing what it thought about him.

So much for that. Now let us run—hastily and superficially indeed—through his books, beginning, since this is an age of fiction, with the novels and stories. There are eleven full-length

ARTIFEX: SKETCHES AND IDEAS

novels, including his re-writing or "re-creation" of Miss Skinner's *The Boy in the Bush;* six short novels or long short stories; and at least fifty short stories of varying length.

I think a clue to the Laurentian novel can be found in his own essay on the novel. (If you really want to read it—none of his cocksure critics has—you will find it in a book queerly called *Reflections on the Death of a Porcupine*.) There he says: "In every great novel, who is the hero all the time? Not any of the characters, but some unnamed and nameless flame behind them all . . . the felt but unknown flame stands behind all the characters, and in their words and gestures there is a flicker of the presence."

The unknown flame in Lawrence's novel is the new vision of the world and of man's relation to it towards which he ceaselessly struggled, sometimes with brilliant clarity, occasionally with perplexed incoherence, but always with interest to the few who will patiently follow him. It is this "hero beyond the characters" which has given rise to the legend that Lawrence "could not draw character," that all his characters are "projections of himself." The former is entirely untrue; the latter only true to the extent that in most of his novels one character is himself. Frieda deceives herself and the truth is not in her when she approvingly quotes her mother's remark that "all his women are you." No. None of the women in *The White Peacock* and *Sons and Lovers* is Frieda; neither is Helena in *The Trespasser;* nor the women in *The Rainbow;* nor Hermione in *Women in Love;* nor Alvina in *The Lost Girl;* nor most of the women in the short stories. But the Ursula in *Women in Love* and *The Rainbow* has bits of Frieda; Tanny in *Aaron's Rod*—a very minor character—is Frieda, and so is Harriet in *Kangaroo*, and Kate in *The Plumed Serpent*.

"Character" as generally understood (if not meant) is little more than exterior information about a person. It may sink as low as some easily recognizable mannerism of speech or

D. H. LAWRENCE

appearance. With Lawrence "character" arises from an intuitive perception of inner reality. For him the novel was not the exposition of a thesis about people, but an adventure of the soul. The ideal of modern society is the "good citizen," whose life on examination proves to be largely a series of legal fictions pivoted on property. Lawrence sought for what is hidden behind this almost universal good-citizen pose. Take marriage —about which Lawrence wrote so much and so earnestly, and in connection with which he has been so wilfully misunderstood and so bitterly maligned. The reality of legal marriage is the existence of signatures on a document, not the infinitely subtle relation of man and woman. It pivots on the idea of property, for it is the property of one in the other which may be injured by the misconduct of husband or wife and judiciously compensated by a money payment. It is a legal fiction. Lawrence was trying to find out and describe what makes a real marriage.

The White Peacock, his first novel, deals with scenes and persons of Lawrence's young days in Derbyshire. Emily, for instance, is a first sketch of the Miriam of *Sons and Lovers*. It is a loosely constructed narrative, showing great power in many individual passages; but Lawrence had not then discovered his genius for organic form. The movement is impeded by a fictitious "I," and the worst fault in the book is a social falsity—he has put working-class people in a middle-class setting. The central character of the book is neither Lettie nor Leslie nor "I," but George, the farmer's son, the tragedy of his broken love for Lettie, his marriage with Meg, his sordid slide into drunkenness. At times the power of evocative writing is superb—among many passages I shall only point to those about London, the feeding of the pigs and the gamekeeper's funeral.

The real "hero" of *The Trespasser* is the Isle of Wight. Under the spell of that vivid writing one seems actually to experience the sea, the sky, the burning sun, the dazzling cliffs and beach, the moon and the mist, the night. The human tragedy of Helena and Siegmund is made poignant by the ambiance of this living beauty of the world. And by contrast it throws up the sordidness of Siegmund's homecoming to his resentful family and of his suicide. Siegmund is not Lawrence, though he has Lawrence's sensibility and experiences; Helena is a perfectly achieved character.

With *Sons and Lovers* Lawrence established himself as a great novelist. When you have experienced that book you have lived through the life of the Morel family and of a Midland mining village in the last generation. You have also lived through the agonies and ecstasies of the young Lawrence striving to win free from his old life. The book is filled with living characters—Walter and Gertrude Morel, Paul (who is Lawrence), Miriam and her family, the pit girls, the factory girls, Clara and Baxter. It is the most readily accessible of Lawrence's novels to a new reader; but he who stops short at *Sons and Lovers* does not know Lawrence. The book contains an almost classical example of the "Œdipus complex," which has been pushed into prominence by the popular vogue for Freudian psychology. It has been used and is still used to decry Lawrence, who is accused of having a "mother complex," a "major neurosis." Now the whole point of the Freudian thesis is that ALL men have an Œdipus complex, just as ALL women have "an Electra complex." Orphans brought up in an institution, who have never seen their fathers and mothers, have it just the same. It is the result of the suppression of certain primitive instincts—the libido—in childhood. The danger of neurosis lies in failure to recognize and face the situation, in keeping it hidden in the unconscious. In Lawrence's case the ideal mother-father of the unconscious were identified with the real father-mother. But he faced the situation and got free. In a sense, he psycho-analyzed himself. He

D. H. LAWRENCE

freed himself from "the terrible mother." It is obvious that the "mother neurosis" detractors are grossly ignorant of the simplest facts about the Freudian theory. The man who supplied the work of art from which this Freudian symbolism is drawn was Sophocles. Does anyone suggest that Sophocles had a "mother neurosis" to any greater or more vicious extent than every man has? Shakespeare's Hamlet faces the same psychological complex as Œdipus and Paul Morel. Had Shakespeare a degenerate "mother neurosis"? Believe me, all this talk about Lawrence's "mother complex" (as if it were something unique and vicious in him) is not only utterly false psychology, it is rot.

The Rainbow and *Women in Love* are closely related, for one is to some extent the sequel to the other. Here Lawrence penetrated deeply into the secrets of human personality, so deeply that the characters often lose much of their exterior reality. *The Rainbow* is planned on a large scale—the history of the succeeding generations of the Brangwens. At times it is tough reading, at times one is a little lost in the generations; but the book contains profound and beautiful writing, and is of cardinal importance for a real understanding of the Lawrentian novel. *Women in Love* is lighter, and is the most popular of his novels—perhaps on account of the title. It is poised round the life of Ursula Brangwen, but contains much of Lawrence's own experience—he himself comes in as Birkin. In this book he relies less on memory and more on immediate experience. Hence the cry—popularized by Norman Douglas, who was peeved by the portrait of himself as Argyle in *Aaron's Rod*—of "putting people" into his books. I was a bit peeved myself when Lawrence made me into one of his undistinguished minor characters—I thought I at least deserved a whole book.

Lawrence was finishing the first draft of *Women in Love* when he was brought up short by the silly and vindictive prosecution and suppression of *The Rainbow*. The whole

ARTIFEX: SKETCHES AND IDEAS

stupid business makes me sick to think of, so I won't go into it. For my immediate purpose it is enough to remark that it stopped his novel writing for a considerable period, and diverted him from one of his great purposes—exploring the hinterland of human consciousness. *The Lost Girl* and *Aaron's Rod* are much more on the surface of life. *The Lost Girl* indeed is almost as shallow as an Arnold Bennett novel in its opening. It comes vividly alive at the end when Alvina and Cicio—a marvellous portrait of an Italian, by the way—leave England for Italy. Aaron also goes to Italy. There is this much truth in the "personal projection" sneer that Lawrence's characters are made to share his destiny. They could scarcely do otherwise. The Italian scenes in both these novels are beautifully done, and the picture of the "vicious old maids" society in Florence (*Aaron's Rod*) is not only essentially true, it is most amusing comedy. Lilley and Aaron are two aspects of Lawrence, though Aaron is unsatisfactorily tangled up with someone else. Implied or expressed in both these novels is the rejection of English society and English values.

Three full-length novels remain. *Kangaroo* contains Lawrence's wonderfully sensitive experience of the Australian country and his real and imaginary experiences with Australians. Once more we are made to see how modern society has no place either for the poet or the essential natural man. Lawrence-Somers is quite prepared to take his place in Australian life. Some of the Australians have heard of him, and are flattered. They are quite prepared to make use of him. But how? As propagandist for some futile political movement. Between Willie the bolshie, and 'Roo and Jack the digger-fascists, Somers has a pretty time. When he refuses to be implicated by either, Jack turns round, insults him odiously, and can think of no explanation except that Somers is a spy! (This was particularly insulting as the war idiots in England thought Lawrence a spy.) Another sapient Australian advises

D. H. LAWRENCE

Somers-Lawrence not to invest money in the country. A hopeless *gâchis*—nothing to do but get out. Somers gets, not pleased with right-you-are-right-ho democracy. The book contains a retrospective chapter about Lawrence's experiences during the war—a wonderfully vivid and sustained piece of writing. But don't miss the interpretations of the place, Australia.

The Plumed Serpent is a difficult book. I'm not sure that I yet understand it. Superficially it relates the adventures of an Englishwoman in Mexico, who gets mixed up with revolutionaries and finally marries one of them. Don Ramon and Cipriano are a sort of mystical fascists, basing themselves not on business but on a revival of worship of the old Mexican gods. There is much curious ritual and a lot of free verse poems, which again I don't understand. As a matter of fact, I find it rather hard to believe in Don Ramon and Cipriano, especially Cipriano. He has a most un-Latin disregard for money. The value of the book to me lies in the pictures of Mexican life and country.

Lady Chatterley's Lover is available in England only in a castrated form which destroys most of its point. It turns on a favourite idea of Lawrence's—that upper-class Englishmen are duffers with their women, who have to go to foreigners or outcasts or the working-class for their "fulfilment." The girl in *The Virgin and the Gipsy* turns to a gipsy as Lady Chatterley turns to the gamekeeper. In *St. Mawr* there seems nothing but a horse or solitude for the poor woman. In *The Ladybird* a foreign count must make up for the English husband's deficiencies. Then Lawrence turns round and satirizes his own idea in *The Princess* and *The Woman Who Rode Away*. It's no good a woman just going off with a wild man if it's a pose, if there's no reality in the relation. Even with the few who accepted him he was constantly meeting with the difficulty that they stupidly accepted—and tried to imitate—the letter of what he said and not the spirit. How patiently he tried and tried again to explain!

ARTIFEX: SKETCHES AND IDEAS

Particularly in his later years Lawrence was deeply occupied with the problem of finding some new orientation of the religious instinct outside Christianity. He was instinctively a Heraclitian, a believer in the Many and the Flux, though even to the end of his life he still seems to refer to the monotheistic God. Characteristically, he dealt with the problem in these terms—that a right religious attitude had once been possessed by men, had been lost, and must be recovered. A work on these lines which cannot but be displeasing to the orthodox is *The Man Who Died*. Jesus did not really die on the cross; he escaped from the tomb and slowly recovered health in a peasant's hut—a great piece of writing—and in his meditations repudiates his idealistic love teaching; in the second part he wanders and finds reality.

Already I have more than occupied the space allotted to me, yet I have done no more than fringe the subject of Lawrence as a writer with the most cursory summaries of his novels. There are many other books of his to be explored, which MUST be explored by anyone who wishes to know this writer thoroughly. To begin with, there are four volumes of short stories. *The Prussian Officer, England My England, The Woman Who Rode Away* and *The Lovely Lady*. There are those who prefer them to his novels on the ground that they are less diffuse and by their nature compel him to avoid digression. Personally, I don't find Lawrence's novels diffuse, and some of his digressions I think extremely valuable. And while I can read all his short stories with pleasure, none gives me the satisfaction and pleasure of his novels. Among the best to my taste are *The Prussian Officer, The Shades of Spring, Odour of Chrysanthemums, The Horse Dealer's Daughter, Two Blue Birds, The Woman Who Rode Away, Jimmy and the Desperate Woman, Glad Ghosts, Rawdon's Roof* and *The Man Who Loved Islands*. Those familiar with the short stories will see that my preference goes to the slightly satiric little comedies.

D. H. LAWRENCE

Along with Norman Douglas—though in a totally different style—Lawrence stands very high as a writer of travel books. Douglas writes from the truth of long and close association with places and a formidable documentation; Lawrence from the truth of immediate sensitive contact. The essays in *Twilight in Italy* show amazing intuitive insight and his invariable response to beauty that was new to him. On a first reading it is well to skip the "philosophical" digressions. Out of many admirable pages I shall mention only the masterly analysis of the dullness of Zurich and the portraits of Paolo and his family. If there are still any who think Lawrence couldn't "draw character" they should read these absolutely sure portraits of Paolo, Maria, Giovanni and Marco. Douglas himself has never given Italian character more understandingly—he is too inclined to use his wits against the peasant instead of his sympathy to understand him.

Sea and Sardinia is almost a *tour de force* of making much out of little. It describes—but how brilliantly!—a train journey from Taormina to Palermo, a ship journey to Cagliari, three days' train and bus travel in Sardinia, the return to Civita Vecchia, to Rome and Naples, and the boat journey back to Sicily. That is all, and it is a masterpiece, giving more of the essence of lower class life in Italy than any book I know. I have been over most of the itinerary at different times, and know how true and alive Lawrence's descriptions are.

Mornings in Mexico again consists of essays; they were written at the top of his form as a writer. Every one of them is good, but I particularly like the one about the Indian servant, the dog and the parrots, the two about the Indian dances, and his reminiscences of the ranch in New Mexico written in Italy. Apropos this book I cannot help referring to a fatuous criticism of it by a really fine writer who should have known better. He accuses Lawrence of "infantilism" because he (Lawrence) casually mentions that he is writing out of doors "in an exercise book."

ARTIFEX: SKETCHES AND IDEAS

There is great and pointless merriment about the little pupil. But what in the name of sanity was the man to write in out of doors? Loose sheets would blow about. He had to have a blank book. And when you buy them, when I buy them, we ask for "exercise books." In any case, even if the critic had been right, which he wasn't, what a fearfully trivial point! Not worth making.

Etruscan Places consists of essays. It is complete so far as it goes, but Lawrence intended to visit and write about other Etruscan towns besides the four dealt with. Chiusi, Cortona, Perugia and Orvieto are among the omissions. We need not regret this too much, since he included Volterra the most magnificently situated of the Etruscan towns, and Tarquinia which contains the best painted tombs. He documented this book carefully—I possess two or three of his source books, which include the best modern Italian authority—and refers to the Vatican and Florence collections of Etruscan art. But he seems to have overlooked the Villa Papa Julia which contains the most superb of all Etruscan terracottas, the Apollo of Veii. The reader need not fear a technical book; there is plenty of the Laurentian "human" touch, and nearly as much about Luigi, the Maremma peasant, and the grouchy young German savant, as about the Etruscans. I am quite sure the scientific people would say Lawrence's Etruscans are fanciful, his interpretation of the tomb symbolism gratuitous; and I am equally sure that Lawrence makes the Etruscans seem alive and interesting in a way no archæologist—not even Dennis—has done. I don't mean to disparage Dennis, his book is greater than Lawrence's in its own way, but he hadn't Lawrence's innate gift of poetical interpretation.

The remaining prose works include two short books, *Psychoanalysis and the Unconscious*, and *Fantasia of the Unconscious*, which are better left alone until the reader is well soaked

D. H. LAWRENCE

in the Laurentian mood and peculiar phraseology. I think that eventually they will be regarded as important, but they need close reading, very careful analysis and skilful interpretation. All I need say is that there is nothing innately absurd—as some people seem to think—in the Laurentian theory of the physiological basis of the unconscious. It is held by some very respectable German psychologists, who formulated the theory scientifically after Lawrence had stated it more poetically from his own intuition. Rather in the same category are the essays in *Reflections on the Death of a Porcupine*, to which I have already referred. *Apocalypse*, a posthumous book, is a new interpretation of Revelation, where Lawrence restates some of his religious ideas in terms more accessible to the unprepared reader. The book is important also for the light it throws on the symbolism of his latest poems, which are otherwise rather obscure at times.

Studies in Classical American Literature and *Assorted Articles* show Lawrence in the unexpected *rôle* of literary critic and newspaper journalist. Naturally, neither the criticism nor the journalism is of an ordinary sort. The criticism is the reverse of pompous—in fact it is at times a little too flip and *en pantoufles*. But it contains a series of very original interpretations of standard American writers, from Franklin to Whitman. It is a much better book than is generally allowed, and contains a lot of truth as well as some rather witty writing. *Assorted Articles* contains very typical comments on miscellaneous subjects, including a short article about his own life as a writer. I think he is wrong in attributing his loneliness to class feeling; it was the inevitable loneliness of the remarkable man, the genius. Byron and Burns were just as lonely.

Before leaving this miscellaneous prose, I must mention the *Introduction to the Memoirs of M.M.* Whatever your view of that transaction—and there is a perfectly good case for Lawrence—it is impossible to deny the high quality of the writing. Norman Douglas acknowledges this handsomely in his

ARTIFEX: SKETCHES AND IDEAS

Magnus-Lawrence pamphlet where he complains that Lawrence wasn't a gentleman. One among several answers is: Neither were Benvenuto Cellini and Villon and a good many others who yet were great artists.

Except for *David* I think Lawrence's plays negligible. The matter of *A Collier's Friday Night* appears to better advantage in *Sons and Lovers;* and the theme of the *Widowing of Mrs. Holroyd* comes out more dramatically in the story, *Odour of Chrysanthemums.*

Lawrence would be ranked far higher as a poet if he had written nothing but poetry. He suffers from the usual fate of polygraphs—people are too lazy-minded to include a large varied mass of creative writing. And contemporary criticism of poetry is so narrow-minded and pedantic that it hasn't begun to understand Lawrence's poems. He is not a great poet, but he is a very good one. He cannot be attached to any particular "school," though he picked up some of his technique from the "Georgians" and for his later work from the writers of free verse. He seldom used rhyme and conventional metre after about 1916. I particularly recommend the poems originally published under the title of *Birds, Beasts and Flowers* and the poems found in MS. "A" of *Last Poems,* which lead up to and include *Ship of Death* and the other poems written when he was dying. They have great poignancy and beauty.

Now that I have finished this pamphlet I am chiefly conscious of its inadequacy; but Lawrence's writings cannot be dealt with properly except at book length. All I have attempted to do is to give some of his obvious (and mostly overlooked) qualities as a writer, and to make the briefest *catalogue raisonnée* of the books. The pamphlet will have entirely succeeded in its purpose if it induces even a few members of the public *to read Lawrence,* instead of reading books about him, idiotic and malevolent newspaper comment, and the even more idiotic and malevolent comment of pseudo-intellectuals, neither of which class has read him. If you must have the personal side, there are his *Letters*.

Tobago, 1935.

P.S. The reader can scarcely have failed to notice that these notes on Lawrence's books are in many cases too rapid and over-condensed. The circumstances and purpose for which the notes were written will explain though not excuse these defects. When recently Messrs. Heinemann took over the complete works of D. H. Lawrence they asked me to write some sort of introductory pamphlet to be given away in bookshops with the purpose of arousing interest in the books. Their opinion was that too much attention has been given to the merely personal side of Lawrence, with the result that many people talk glibly about him without ever having read more than two or three of his own writings, which after all are what really matter. With this I entirely agreed, and gladly wrote the pamphlet. But I was absolutely limited as to space, and for this reason could not treat the books as fully as I should have done if there had been no such conditions. I had to do the best I could and always to bear in mind that I was attempting to persuade indifferent members of the public to read a dead author. The pamphlet has been included in the American edition of this book because while I have heard opinions about Lawrence expressed by numerous Americans I have yet to meet one who has read all his books. I hope I may be forgiven for saying that in the absence of that elementary requirement I could not think the opinions expressed had much validity.

R. A.

Sea Travel

Sea Travel

FROM the train England looked grey and unhappy under a veiled sky, in February frost. There was only enough frost to give it stiffness, not enough to make a sparkle of rime. At midday there seemed scarcely enough light to make a diamond sparkle. All the way to the west a drab uninteresting landscape, just not flat enough to have the majestic monotony of a great plain. And the settlements! Can it be possible, I asked myself, that a great nation which has been so opulent should be housed so meanly, should live in such inæsthetic squalor? At best we make a suburb with railings and auriculas, and rest on the ignominious laurels. I waited impatiently for Bath, a city planned for—I couldn't recollect for what noble purpose Bath had been planned, but at any rate it had been planned, it wasn't an industrial excrescence. But alas, from the railway Bath looked smoke-grimed and mean. It had evidently seen better days and had no hope of their returning. The haphazard meanness of it all! A Frenchman would have been delighted with these reiterated evidences of *spleen*. But I am not French, and the dingy meanness of my own country oppressed me.

I was unfair, I knew I was unfair. I knew that in sheltered nooks the long slender sallows would be furred with golden buds, and that though the hazel catkins would hang droopily in that dun air they would be golden too. I knew that at least some of those sad-looking coppices concealed fragile white anemones, some with just a tinge of pink or faint purple, enough to remind one of their kinship with their more splendid cousins, the bright blue and purple anemones of the south. I knew there would be early primroses, and perhaps part of a hillside whitened with snowdrops. But the train went too fast or I was unlucky—not the glimpse of a flower the whole way, only an insipid uninteresting lunch in the restaurant car, the essence of philistinism in food. And once more I could not help but be glad to leave. Who was it said that the finest things Englishmen have constructed are the boats which take them away?

Going to sleep that night in the cabin—which was indisputably clean and excellent in point of drainage—I thought of Urbino and Salamanca.

Sea travel is usually held to be both monotonous and unpleasant, a period of empty uncomfortable days to be got through somehow and anyhow. This is no doubt true of cold, wet and very windy weather; but not of other times. I have spent happy, even enchanted hours and days on Italian and French ships in the Mediterranean. Very pleasant to leave Venice for Brindisi in the afternoon, and to watch the lovely dead city slowly fade in the distance across the green Adriatic. Still pleasanter—though it is not a sea journey at all—is the little trip over the lagoon past Malamocco to Chioggia, with the sun so warm over the shimmering still water as one watches the low islands and the long strip of the Lido and the black piles marking the ship track and the coloured sails of the fishing boats all slowly gliding past in a bright dream. Lovely, always, to sail in or out of the gulf of Naples, to see the straits of Messina, to make Palermo in the early morning, to coast along to Trapani past the mountainous headlands, or to see the bare mountains near Tunis red in the red dawn. Good, too, the long

SEA TRAVEL

blue journey from Algiers to Marseilles, which bright as it is looks colourless after the desert light. I remember with happiness the four days from Tilbury to Lisbon—the cloud shadows over the long estuary, a silvery grey Kent under mist while we were in sunlight, the sudden unfamiliar sea view of the familiar South Foreland, Boulogne at evening with the lights coming out, Cap Ushant the next evening, coming into Vigo Bay before dawn under quiet stars, the gorse-covered mountain coast on the way to Leixoẽs, and then the Tagus. Best of all the enchanted days from Naples along the Italian coast, past Capraea and Monte Cristo and Elba, and Corsica in the evening, the golden isles of Hyères at dawn, with a sea glimpse of the vigie on Port Cros, where we lived happy weeks.

No, I can't say that I find sea travel unpleasant or even monotonous. On a ship I don't want to do anything except passively live the hours of sky and sea as they move slowly by. One who was charmed into ecstasy among green solitudes was said by the Greeks to be rapt away by the nymphs, a nympholept; but I don't remember that they ever spoke of the sea rapture. Probably in their flimsy craft the sea was too near and terrible; they had to be unceasingly active and vigilant. But in our large safe ships we can easily contemplate ourselves into a sea ecstasy—if only our fellow passengers will allow us. But will they?

"We have lost the sense of wonder," says Yeats. And he is right. Yet I think he is wrong in wanting us to wonder over obsolete marvels, rather silly old tales of fairies and spirits and dead heroes. What is Conchubar to us who have lived with real warriors? Only the *citadin* thinks war romantic. Even the siege of Troy was a sordid affair—Homer lets us see it—with intrigues of commanders and squabbles over booty. Yeats, I think, would revive a false sense of wonder. We should give wonder and reverence to the familiar elemental things, the things the *citadin* takes for granted or never thinks of. There are

ARTIFEX: SKETCHES AND IDEAS

such different ways of "knowing." For so long now men have thought of knowing as establishing dominion through analysis; the weight, distance, motion, chemical composition of the stars, for instance. What have they to do with the wonder of a starry sky? It is the living wonder of the stars we need to know; and the living cannot be analyzed. The dominion of science is a very real thing, but it disintegrates the living impulse. It is better to be in harmony with the living world than to establish ourselves as a set of cocksure Canutes from whom the waves will really retire at a word.

I shouldn't like to live on a ship; men are essentially land creatures, needing the smell and taste of earth. The potency of naked sea and sky is too terrific, and by contrast brings out too painfully the little human relations in the floating prison. The sea mood is not inhuman, but it is non-human. One is saturated hour after hour in powerful non-human influences—the gold-white sunlight, the blue-white air, the blue-green water dashed ceaselessly with foam. Establish a harmony with these, and human interests—real too in their place—become an intrusion, a discord. In the sea mood I don't want to discuss politics and novels and rates of exchange. . . .

It is wonderful that we live in so coloured a world. To see the colours fade in the twilight is always a little unhappy, and there is always a sense of exultation when they come back brighter and brighter with the dawn. To be up at dawn is one of the privileges of humanity, which it seldom enjoys. Still more wonderful is the simple taken-for-granted fact that our sky is blue. It is such an incomparable background for the coloured earth, and stains the colourless sea with such variety of fluid blues and greens. How ghastly if our sky and sea were red—we could never exist in such a world—or if our sun glared like a white furnace mouth from a black sky. Yet there are such worlds. I will say nothing of the wonder of clouds, like heavy foam on the blue sky; or the wonder of foam, like thin ravelled

SEA TRAVEL

clouds on the blue water. It is not a matter of just seeing them—everyone *sees* them—but of feeling them as things vivid and relevant to one's own life. Those who feel need no telling, and to others it is just ridiculous.

This is not the old pathetic fallacy, but a real experience, more elemental, primitive if you like—coming for a time into touch with essential physical truths and powers. I don't imagine that the sky shares my moods or that the sun loves me. Love is altogether a wrong word—a polluted, debased word. I hate Christian love; it's messy and false. If I fall off a ship in the Atlantic, it won't take many waves to choke me. If I'm fool enough to lie for hours under a fierce sun, he'll peel my nose and make my eyes bloodshot and give me a fever. Living in hot countries makes you respect the sun and keep away from intruding your white belly on him. But then I know if I put my hand in the soft-looking red fire of pine logs I shall be burned; which doesn't prevent my knowing the wonder of fire. And I can feel all through me the wonder of the tiger's strength and striped grace, though he would eat me if he were hungry and could get at me. It is salutary to measure one's unimportance—easy prey for a few tons of sea water or a big cat.

In spite of protests to the contrary, the organized life of this epoch is stiffly against this naked perception of the great elements, this sacred play and happiness. "Environment" they say pompously, but they don't mean the real environment; they mean a street, preferably a suburban street, a room in an office and a cozily furnished room in a suburban house. Those and the people who live in them are "environment," in their meaning. The real environment, the real wonder they want to shut out. They do shut it out. At most they open a window and say how nice Nature is. Nature isn't nice at all. It is tremendous and mysterious, indecent if you like, but not "nice," not a bit "nice." So they worship "Nature" by having neat flower gardens and playing tennis, or more likely shut the window and

ARTIFEX: SKETCHES AND IDEAS

turn on the radio. How detestable is that word "Nature"! A sentimental insult.

On a ship making a longish voyage you realize how eager people are to avoid any real communion with the living environment, how bored they are with it. A modern passenger ship is a mixture of a children's playground and a vulgar hotel where they play a gramophone at meal-times and pretend it's an orchestra. It is all pretentious and false, from the long pretentious menu which furnishes scarcely anything fit to eat but pea-soup and jacket potatoes to the farce of "dressing" and the futility of organized games. At all costs the traveller at sea must be distracted from the sea, never be allowed to feel for a moment the awe of the unimpeded sky and those uncountable leagues of quiet or angry water. So the hours must be killed, quite foully murdered, poor things, by too frequent meals and cocktails and deck tennis and quoits and parlour golf and more cocktails and backgammon and bridge and tiddledewinks and all the rest of it. You may, of course, lie in a deck-chair with a magazine—"I'm such a sun-worshipper, my dear!"—or determinedly and virtuously stamp your twelve or twenty times unseeingly round the deck, "keeping fit." And that is all. So poor in life they are all day. And at night the lovely peace of the swishing water and the soft humming engines and the dim starry darkness must be driven away with jazz, while the women pretend they enjoy dancing on a heaving deck and the men pretend to believe it. How silly and pretentious it all is, and—to me—a soul-crushing boredom.

Well, that is how people are nowadays, that is what they want. I really don't mind much, so long as they leave me alone in my world which suffices me. They seem to me like ants, but terribly noisy, destructive and assertive ants; and the worst of it is they *can't* leave one alone. Any one who quietly ignores their shut-in noisy little world affronts them, and they want to pull him down. How much they resented my silent loitering

SEA TRAVEL

about the ship, ignoring the games, living the sea and the sky! I wouldn't let them pull me in. Yet in the end I did, not so much from weakness as from choice—I don't always like people to hate me. I had had nine days of the sea, and I could feel the land coming near—almost hear the radios making exactly the same noises as in London. So it didn't matter any more. Yet I still wonder why people bother to go on ships, when they could have had all they did have more cheaply and more comfortably by staying at home.

Mrs. Todgers

Mrs. Todgers

❧❧

SHE was a small cat with glossy black fur, a middle-aged figure and eyes like flecked, transparent stones. I can't quite remember why I answered the question: "What shall we call the cat?" by saying: "Mrs. Todgers." Perhaps it was because I had been re-reading *Martin Chuzzlewit*. But I think it was because she was rather in the position of a landlady while, at appropriate times, she was only too willing to get off with any Pecksniff of a tom-cat.

Behind the cottage was a large malt-house, and Mrs. Todgers belonged to a family where the females at least were locally renowned for their mousing qualities. She was one of two or three half-wild cats who lived on the plentiful mice in the old malt-house. Apparently she and she alone—in accordance with mysterious cat law—had a claim to impose herself on the human inhabitants of the cottage. Certainly Mrs. Todgers never allowed us to become familiar with any of the other cats she tolerated quite amiably on the common hunting-ground. If any of them dared to take a short cut across the garden or (still more heinous offence) to sneak into the shed after any scraps the old lady might have left from a meal, there was a row at once, prodigious spittings and growlings, which invariably ended with the ignominious flight of the intruder. On such occasions the usually sleek and dignified Mrs. Todgers bristled up into a black porcupine, and her mysterious eyes glared with all the horrid passions of war.

She was glad to see us, there can be no doubt about that, so glad that for days and days she was quite unable to settle down to the ordinary cat routine of sleeping in the most comfortable chair or blinking at the fire. She had a startling way of appearing suddenly, apparently from nowhere, like a conjuring trick or a manifestation at a séance. Then for hours on end she would stand purring, slowly marking time with her front paws while she affectionately dug her claws deep in the new cocoa-matting. Even when she eventually calmed down sufficiently to be able to sit still and enjoy us, delight would occasionally get the better of her and up she went to her purring tread-mill, regardless of damage to the floor covering.

Why was Mrs. Todgers so glad? Doubtless, our fire, our shelter and our food? Not a bit of it. Mrs. Todgers was an exception to the economic interpretation of history. Mrs. Todgers didn't need any material advantages we could give her: what she wanted was our company, our affection. When she turned up she was not in the haggard, plaintive condition of the half-starved cat. On the contrary she was plump and sleek, and her black coat gleamed with health and repletion. Milk was regularly provided for the malt-house cats, there were two or three houses where they were welcome to beg, and mice abounded; moreover, the malt-house had plenty of snug nooks for dreaming and kittening, and in winter provided a glorious fire of anthracite. As cat economics go, Mrs. Todgers was rich and had no need to ask a favour of anybody. True, she liked her bit of fish or game and called loudly for it when she smelled it on the table, but what hard-working mother ever refused a lunch at the Carlton or a dinner at the Savoy? These little treats were exceptions in a virtuous life.

No, what Mrs. Todgers wanted was not economic advan-

MRS. TODGERS

tage, but a woman's life—a quiet home and a good steady man about the place. It was some time before I found it out, but Mrs. Todgers chose me as the good steady man—a flattering but occasionally onerous situation. While I pledge my word of honour that I had absolutely nothing to do with the kittens she produced with such appalling rapidity and regularity, I can also assert than in almost every other respect she treated me more as a husband than as a friend. As far as I could see, there was practically no limit to the various offices she felt she had a right to demand of me.

At first Mrs. Todgers was timid and admitted no familiarity beyond a formal stroking and a slight scratch under the chin; but this only goes to show that the French are right—*les grandes passionnées sont timides*. Gradually Mrs. Todgers extended her empire over me and began (forgive the impropriety of the confession) by sitting on my knee when I was reading. In those days I did a great deal of reading, so Mrs. Todgers had a maximum of opportunity. Appearing with her usual mysterious suddenness, she would leap lightly on to my thigh and retain her balance, in spite of my involuntary start, by digging her claws firmly into my flesh. When I had yelled and removed them, she would gradually settle down to a long-distance purr, with her head over my knee, occasionally sticking her claws into me with voluptuous intensity. Had I been a masochist, this would have been delicious, but since I wasn't, I had to implore her to stop.

When, at last, she settled down to doze and I attempted to return to my book, complications began. Try holding your leg still with a plump pussy asleep on it, and see if you don't get pins and needles. The slightest movement on my part brought a sharp reminder from two sets of claws and a loud, reproachful purring. Moreover, I was chained to my seat—impossible to get up and make a note or consult a reference book or drink a glass of water or perform any of the necessary fidgets of the

ARTIFEX: SKETCHES AND IDEAS

sedentary worker. If I did any of these things, what angry looks, what indignant twitchings of a domineering tail! It was even worse if I sacrificed her to "My Art," and resolutely dumped her to go to the writing-table—she would leave the room precipitately waving a tail which spoke volumes, and refuse to have anything to do with me for the rest of the day.

Mrs. Todgers frankly disapproved of my writing; there wasn't enough room between the lap and the wood, and the movements of writing interrupted her doze. From time to time she would turn a sleepy eye up at me, evidently remarking: "My good man, *must* you do this sort of thing?"

As for typing, Mrs. Todgers couldn't bear it. Directly the hideous rattle started, she also would start to her feet, look wildly round and make a flying leap for the door.

The writing-table, then, had disagreeable associations for her, and she usually kept away from it. Sometimes I would find two or three muddy paw marks on a piece of clean manuscript, but this was evidently only done to show her good will, to prove to me that in spite of her housewifely scorn of it all, her affection was great enough for her to take an interest in my weird hobbies.

Whenever I saw those paw marks, I said to myself: "Ah, yes, men are just great big children who have to be humoured sometimes."

I'm sure that's what Mrs. Todgers thought.

Among the various demonstrations of her feelings there was one I always deprecated and tried vainly to avoid. Through the silence of my library a brittle, scratching noise would be heard —merely Mrs. Todgers idly sharpening her claws on the back of one of my folios.

"Mrs. Todgers!"

Languidly she would desist, look fixedly at me, yawn vigorously, stretch her fore-legs and arch her back, and then sweep out like a lady. Nothing could induce her to break this affectionate custom of preferring my books to the gate-post or a tree. *Beyle's Dictionary*, I remember, lost the labels and most of the gold tooling from its four vast folios; and a precious *Liddell and Scott* had to be moved to another shelf. But perhaps Mrs. Todgers was here playing the part of Nemesis, punishing me for having torn some of my father's books in my inept infancy.

Even more embarrassing favours were to come. Mrs. Todgers was as keen a huntress as Diana herself, and, what's more, she was a poacher. Rabbits. More than once have I seen her, head high and every muscle strained, dragging through the morning dew a rabbit as big as herself. I always dreaded that the keepers would get her sooner or later, but they never did; she was an artful old dodger.

The partly devoured carcasses of these rabbits were to me an embarrassment. Mrs. Todgers ate every bit of them, always beginning with the nose and ending with the tail, sickeningly crunching and gulping her awful festival of Trimalchio. During these periodic gorges her belly was as fat and hard as if she had swallowed a croquet ball—her left side bulged with rabbit. Her capacity for eating rabbit was indeed prodigious, but huge as it was, she could never eat more than half a rabbit at a sitting. The problem for her was what to do with the disgusting relics, while she lapped river water, dozed and digested. Obviously if she left them outside, they would be raided by other cats while she was asleep by the fire.

Mrs. Todgers solved this problem by bringing the half-eaten corpse for me to guard. When you are writing a life of Voltaire, and feeling worked up about the tremendous conflict of good and evil in human destiny, it is disconcerting to have half a bloody rabbit gently deposited on your foot. That is what Mrs. Todgers did to me, looking up and uttering a very faint mew, which she always turned on in moments of stress and emotion. Plainly she took for granted that it was my job to look after her leavings. I tried the device of putting the horrid thing in the garden with the tongs, but she immediately brought it back. There was nothing to do but wrap it hastily in the *Times* and put the nasty bundle hastily in the waste-paper basket. After sniffing round the basket and uttering a few monitory mews, she would appear satisfied and sit dreamily before the fire, statuesque as an Egyptian, occasionally hitching her behind a little closer to the genial warmth.

Usually a couple of days elapsed before she finally disposed of her rabbit, for appetite was less keen than immediately after the kill. After each meal the diminished remains were brought back to me for safe keeping. Once I tested her altruism. While she was asleep I gave the half-rabbit to another cat, and when Mrs. Todgers asked for it I pretended I had eaten it myself. She sniffed very carefully all round the basket, looking up at me inquiringly from time to time. I expected dismal complaints and a withdrawal of future confidence. But, no. Deciding that I must have eaten it, she rubbed herself affectionately against my leg, purring loudly, went to sleep and never asked for the rabbit again. I assumed, perhaps fatuously, that she was quite willing for me to have my share; and in any case she continued bringing me fragments of future rabbits.

Nobody who has been owned by a female cat will feel inclined to dispute the statement that Mrs. Todgers was a fertile mother of generations. She was a menace to the balance of nature. At least 75 per cent. of her offspring had to be exposed in early infancy, and we should have had trouble in finding homes for the remnant but for Mrs. Todgers' renown as a mouser which descended to her female children. Anyone who has seen the Forum of Trajan, that sad dungeon of destitute cats, will have to agree that this wholesale murder of squawking kittens is preferable to an excess in the cat population. I took the moral responsibility for the murders, but I was glad to shelve the actual deed on to others. This was performed by a cottager, a mild and amiable man with several children. He refused to take any reward, because, he said, he liked drowning kittens. One has strange and frightening glimpses of human nature even in a small village.

A comfortable basket, lined with hay and part of an old woollen garment, was provided for Mrs. Todgers' frequent maternities in the place she seemed to like—the semi-darkness of the coal and wood shed. The shattering thing about it was that I had to be present. The event was announced by uneasy wanderings and loud purring, varied by the mute and appealing mew I have mentioned. That mew meant Mrs. Todgers wanted me to do something. I would pour her milk, which she refused, smooth her fur and make amiable noises which she accepted, but wherever I went there she was, looking up and uttering that strange mew. Time and again I would go to the basket with her at my heels, wait until she seemed comfortably installed, and then tiptoe away. In two minutes there she was again—mew, mew, mew, so faint and gentle, but how devilishly insistent. I was afraid she would do herself a mischief, wandering about at such a time, and I didn't want her to bring forth on the carpet at my feet. There was nothing else to do—I had to bring a chair and sit beside her in the coal-shed until a crescendo of purring informed me that I could at last depart. Meanwhile, sitting there between the mother and the coal, I had plenty of time to meditate on birth and death, the geology of the Carboniferous age, Lawrence, and the life of coal-miners.

Acting on the theory that only children are unhappy, we rashly preserved two of the first litter produced by Mrs. Todgers under our auspices. The children were happy enough, but in the exuberance of their youth they devastated the garden and committed excesses in the house. Thereafter one only was kept, theory or no theory. But though I deplored her reckless fecundity, I gladly admit that Mrs. Todgers was a good mother. When they were little, she would bring a specially good one in to show me, watch its blind sprawlings with a sentimental eye, and then, satisfied with compliments and caresses, carry it back. As the one survivor grew up, she took uncommon pains with its education. Holding it down with one paw, in spite of squeals and struggles, she taught it to wash by licking it until its fur shone. She taught it to fight and endure pain by sparring with it and nipping it until it howled and fled in terror behind a cupboard. She showed it how to be clean, and cuffed it when it misbehaved. At exactly the right moment she would appear with a live mouse, uttering a particular hunting call reserved for these occasions. It was interesting to see the kitten. Bristling with joy and ferocity, it would leap on the mouse, caper, curvet, rush about, crouch and spring, and finally worry the unhappy captive to death while Mrs. Todgers looked on with benevolent blinks. A happier spectacle was to watch her teaching a kitten how to climb a post and how to jump on to the fence, doing it gracefully herself first and then pretending complete indifference while she watched the kitten's clumsy imitations from the corner of one eye.

The Abbé Pluche, who believed in Providence, tells us that melons are marked in sections, so that they may be equitably divided in large families. I don't know how he accounted for cats, which have succeeded in imposing themselves on humanity without supplying essential needs like the sheep, cow and horse, and without employing any of the abject flattery and docility of the dog. Many animals, even seals, can be induced to perform tricks, but not a cat. Has anyone ever seen performing cats? I suppose they have existed, but they must be rare. Cats are like donkeys and camels, they won't ever quite give in to human tyranny, they won't try to imitate the human soul. Independent beasts—you won't get them to play *God Save the King* with their noses. Probably the Abbé would have said that Providence created cats in order to keep down the mice; which seems rough luck on the mice, which must therefore have been created by Providence in order to be kept down by the cats.

A dog will sometimes gulp down a bit of food he doesn't like in order to please you. Not a cat—she'll see you blowed first. I have seen cats eat olives and asparagus, but no other vegetable except a little mashed potato, if there is butter in it. Mrs. Todgers was no exception. She wouldn't do tricks, and you might coax her till the cows came home—she wouldn't eat what she didn't want to eat. It was the same with her hunting. I once disturbed her sleep to carry her off to a chicken run, where I had seen a young rat. She, the exterminator of rodents, saw it at once, watched it running frantically about, yawned and walked away. The lesson was plain—Mrs. Todgers would hunt at her own whim, not at mine.

I don't in the least admire sportsmen, have a contempt for them in fact, but I did admire old Mrs. Todgers. She never bothered to boast about mice, but judging from her reputation, her wonderful coat, her slender appetite for scraps and the numbers of mice she brought her children, she must have been an unerring huntress. In the season the paths were strewn with the corpses of shrew mice she had killed and disdained to eat.

I have already mentioned her prowess among rabbits. She was also a ratter, and I've seen her nail a rat which was putting up fight in a corner when many a dog would have funked. One morning she brought me two monstrous great rats, each neatly killed with a nip in the neck. Nor did she ever turn tail from a hostile dog, however confident and fierce-looking. My neighbours' cocker spaniels knew better than ever to enter the garden—you couldn't get them past the gate. And I have seen a walloping retriever fly howling with a bloody nose after one vicious dab from Mrs. Todgers.

She was as agile as she was brave. One summer day I was sitting in a garden-chair and Mrs. Todgers was washing her face by the gate. The fence was about three feet high, and there was thick ivy on the wall where the fence joined it. A sparrow flew across the garden, hovered by the ivy, about six inches above the fence end, saw Mrs. Todgers and turned to escape. Too late. From her sitting position she sprang straight in the air, caught the sparrow in her mouth, and landed with it on the other side of the fence. I've never seen anything quite so quick.

Equally impressive and more courageous was her manner of dealing with a large adder. She had a litter of young kittens at the time, which perhaps accounts for it. We returned from a walk and saw Mrs. Todgers dabbing at something which was squirming on a flower bed. It was an adder, already helpless with a broken spine and covered with deep gashes from those merciless claws. Mrs. Todgers took no notice of us. She was like a concentrated mass of steel springs. Keeping cautiously out of range of its writhing head, she watched the adder intently. Every now and then her right paw shot out and back like a boxer's arm and there was another deep gash in the adder's body. She kept breaking its spine inch by inch, until she got right to the head and only its tail moved. Then she sat calmly but intently beside it, and watched until it was dead hours later. Then, after a few final dabs just to make sure, she left it and returned to her kittens. What impressed me was the combination of extreme caution with dexterity of attack. One false movement bringing her within range of the adder's teeth, and Mrs. Todgers would have been dead. She seemed quite aware of the danger, but not for a moment did she funk it.

Her death, after six or seven years living with us, was a sad affair. One day she began following me about, looking up with that silent mew, which meant something was wrong. No kittens were due, no bit of rabbit had to be guarded, and I stupidly thought she was fooling. But the complaints went on. Picking her up a little later, I noticed that two of her breasts were swollen and that touching them seemed to hurt her. She was put into a basket and taken to the vet., who immediately gave a bad report. It was a malady incident to old lady cats, he said, and there was nothing to be done about it. Since she couldn't be cured and was almost certainly in pain, he advised the lethal chamber.

I have often thought about it since, and have wondered if I did right in consenting. That cat trusted me. Did I betray the trust? Perhaps I ought to have given her a few more weeks to see if she would recover, perhaps I ought to have consulted another vet. Sometimes my conscience is troubled, and not altogether quietened by the thought that if I had cancer, I should be only too grateful to anybody who would gas me painlessly.

It will be seen that I am not of those who believe that "man owes no duty to the lower animals." On the contrary, I think that the "higher" men are the more they are conscious of responsibility to creatures who ask their protection and friendship. Among the many disheartening events of our time is the extermination of rare and beautiful animals or their reduction to insignificant numbers, in the name of "sport." Dampier relates that when he and his men landed on a Pacific island, the multitudes of sea-birds were so friendly that they allowed themselves to be picked up and caressed; but, he adds significantly, they soon learned we were their enemies. That is the chief lesson animals have learned from men. Having taught them that bitter truth, we exclaim at the ferocity of the bigger and stronger species and heroically arm to "protect" ourselves. Could we hear their version, it would certainly be a different one.

Cet animal est très méchant;
Quand on l'attaque, il se défend.

La Fontaine's irony puts the whole case in a few words. Cyrano de Bergerac (the real one) imagines himself lost in the land of birds, where he is tried for his life as a public enemy. Bird justice being superior to that of men, he is acquitted as an individual, though the bird justices make cogent remarks on human behaviour.

I have seen it stated that man is the only animal which practices cruelty. After watching Mrs. Todgers with live mice I can't altogether agree. But animals rarely kill for the sake of killing, they kill only for food. Except when incited by men, they do not fight for the sake of fighting. Bison and wild cattle organize for defence, but do not make war on each other. Wild animals avoid each other, and very seldom attack men unless first attacked or frightened. "Nature red in tooth and claw" is true enough, but in nature there is no civil war such as men have practised for many centuries. And if man is so much "higher," as he boasts, then the greater his crime—he ought to know better.

Sentimentality about animals is disgusting, like all sentimentality, which is simply false feeling. And there is a good deal of it in England. But that does not justify the extermination of animal life which is going on so rapidly. I have read in some zoological magazine that unless immediate steps are taken, about forty species of animals will become extinct in Europe alone in the next two decades. Animals are helpless against human arms and human cunning. It rests entirely with us whether our landscapes are to be warm with that intense vivid life or motionless deserts, which they very nearly are already. I owe a debt to Mrs. Todgers, for she taught me that we lose something in life if we miss the chance of friendship with animals. It is more fun than killing them. And I will risk the chance of being accused of misanthropy and of preferring the company of inferiors by saying that I should like a world where there were more animals and fewer human brutes.